YOURS,

A HANDBOOK OF CHRIST

Mowbray Parish Handbooks

YOURS, LORD

A HANDBOOK OF CHRISTIAN STEWARDSHIP

Michael Wright

MOWBRAY

Mowbray
A Cassell imprint
Villiers House, 41/47 Strand, London WC2N 5JE
387 Park Avenue South, New York, NY 10016–8810

First published 1992

British Library Cataloguing-in-Publication Data
A catalogue record for this book is available from the British Library.

Library of Congress Cataloging-in-Publication Data
Available from the Library of Congress.

ISBN 0–264–67275–5

Cartoon by Philip Spence © CCBI

Typeset by Colset Private Limited, Singapore
Printed and bound in Great Britain by
Biddles Ltd, Guildford and King's Lynn

Contents

To Gillian

The Lord God said, 'It is not good for the man to be alone; I shall make a partner suited to him.'

Genesis 2.18

Forewords

When Mowbray first approached the Central Stewardship Committee of the Church of England, I was pleased that the Stewardship Advisers and Resources Officers in the dioceses responded positively and made practical contributions from their own experience.

This book is the result of that initiative, and I welcome it both as a valuable theological and biblical basis for stewardship and as a collection of much practical wisdom.

I warmly commend it to all Christians who are thinking afresh about their commitment to the mission of God and their response to the Grace of God in Christ.

✠ Roy Southwark

The Churches' Stewardship Network brings together those with a national responsibility for Christian stewardship in the member churches of the Council of Churches for Britain and Ireland. It continues the work started by the Stewardship Committee of the former British Council of Churches. That work includes arranging occasional conferences on different aspects of stewardship.

One such conference was held in July 1991 at Coleg Harlech on the theme 'Stewardship . . . the Agent of Change'. Some 180 people drawn from twelve of our member churches attended that conference. Michael Wright was invited to Harlech to absorb the week's thinking and discussion and to produce a handbook of Christian stewardship for the churches. The result is *Yours, Lord*.

I commend this handbook to the 30 member churches of CCBI. It offers a fresh and integrated vision of how as Christians we can practise the stewardship of all our resources. It helpfully develops themes set out in the 1980 BCC report *Christian Stewardship in the 1980s*, and its 1988 sequel *Stewards of God's House* dealing particularly with the stewardship of church buildings.

We are indebted to Mowbray for publishing this book as an inspiration and challenge to all our churches.

John Reardon
General Secretary
Council of Churches for Britain and Ireland

Yours, Lord will help its readers to come to a better understanding of the meaning of stewardship, and will encourage them to put what they discover into practice. I warmly commend it.

David Coffey
General Secretary
Baptist Union of Great Britain

No parish should be without copies of this book. Studying it could transform not just people's attitude to Christian giving but their attitude to every aspect of Christian discipleship.

Alwyn Cambrensis
Archbishop of Wales

This new look on Christian stewardship will stimulate the mind and present a blueprint for a gospel-related lifestyle. It cannot fail to challenge.

Commissioner John Larsson
Territorial Commander
Salvation Army

Christian stewardship is one way of describing the essence of our relationship to God. It is not an 'optional extra' for Churches and individuals. I therefore warmly welcome the comprehensive treatment of the subject in this handbook.

The Rt Revd William B. R. Macmillan
Moderator of the General Assembly
Church of Scotland

This book, in challenging the people of God to full Christian stewardship, could be life-changing for individuals and for congregations. No church should be without a copy. As many Christians as possible should read it – if they dare!

Ruth Clarke
Moderator of General Assembly
The United Reformed Church

DO NOT DISTURB

Introduction

Christian stewardship has changed and grown. It is no longer just about planned giving: it is a much broader and richer vision of glad and grateful response to God for all creation. It is a responsible use of our many blessings, material and spiritual.

I hope that many people in positions of responsibility and leadership in local church congregations will find this book helps them to understand, and to communicate to others, this broader and richer vision of Christian stewardship. Researching and writing it has been a journey of discovery for me; I hope reading it may begin a journey of discovery for you.

In many churches it seems a daunting task to rekindle a vision, and encourage folk to pray, work, and celebrate together to enable something of that vision to become a reality. I have tried to earth the vision in practical ideas that can be used in any congregation, large or small.

I believe that few church members these days are familiar enough with the Bible. I therefore give many full quotations, and refer to chapters more than to individual verses. This is in the hope that it may encourage readers to explore their Bibles more adventurously.

I was invited to write this book by Derek Lane, the Adviser in the Diocese of Durham, on behalf of the Christian Stewardship Network of the Council of Churches for Britain and Ireland, and the Christian Stewardship Committee of the Central Board of Finance of the Church of England. I have tried to write a book that meets their requirements, but if it does not, the responsibility is entirely mine.

I have been much helped by suggestions, and by some constructive responses to earlier drafts by many members of those bodies.

I am indebted to all who sent me their comments and helped me to appreciate the nature of my task, particularly Derek Lane, Colin Davey, Nigel Speller, James Barnes, Ian Fisher, Adrian Mann, Michael Harrison, Barry Morgan, Susan Rennison, Clive Barlow, Gary Bennett, Trevor Beedell, and Haydn Veitch. This is a good mix of responses from the Church of England, the Church of Scotland, the Church in Wales, the Methodist and United Reformed Churches.

I am grateful too for the patient and perceptive support given me by Ruth McCurry, Religious Editor, Cassell.

Above all, I am grateful to my wife Gillian for her patience, good humour, support and encouragement throughout the process of writing this book.

Michael Wright

1

What is Christian Stewardship?

Money is a big issue for leaders of Christian congregations. Very few churches ever seem to have enough of it. The amount of time and energy devoted to fund raising in some churches can be so great that it appears to be one of the major preoccupations of the Christian life. The Summer Fete and the Christmas Fair seem almost to be religious festivals in their own right.

However, money can be a touchy subject with many of our members. We tend to be shy about telling other people how much we earn, and even more shy about how much we give.

It is quite common for people to feel that it is appropriate for our clergy and church leaders to have a lot to say about our Christian believing, belonging, and behaving, but not about our Christian financial giving. Indignantly – or uncomfortably – many of us regard that as an invasion of our privacy.

We may have clear ideas about the costs of food, furniture and fun, but quite unrealistic notions of what it costs adequately to pay our clergy and maintain our church premises. So often we don't consider the need to support the caring and outreach work of our church in mission and ministry, at home and abroad.

What is clear is that we can neither maintain our life and witness, nor grow, with the present level of giving in most of our churches.

So money seems to be uppermost in the minds of church leaders when we think about Christian stewardship. For the last 30 years or so churches in this country have been influenced by Planned Giving and Stewardship Campaigns, run at first by business organizations on American lines, and then shortly afterwards by Stewardship Advisers in dioceses, districts and denominations.

The emphasis of much of this has been on programmes with the three keywords of Time, Talents, and Money. The main aim so often seemed to be to cover the church's costs, and ensure that there were enough people to clean the brass, tidy the church grounds, and do all the tasks that enabled the church to function effectively.

The concept has changed

Over the last ten years, the concept of Christian stewardship has changed considerably. It has become a much richer exploration of our beliefs and lifestyle as Christians. It is not so much a means of keeping the wolf from the door of the church, as an opportunity to review the whole life and ethos of the church. Its concern is for the gospel to be lived and celebrated in daily life and in corporate worship and service.

It is no longer some special and separate activity, to be identified with capital letters as 'Christian Stewardship', but stewardship of all resources practised by Christians. We have a perspective on stewardship which is distinctly different from that of people who do not share our Christian faith.

Where a church has rather lost its way, its life and vigour, where instead of a celebration of deep significance there is a tired and sometimes careless routine of worship, then a careful exploration of the meaning of Christian stewardship can be a revivifying experience. And this can happen even when all you set out to do is to get out of debt.

Where a church is numerically successful, and rather pleased with itself, then a careful exploration of the meaning of Christian stewardship can be a chastening experience, bringing a fresh look at what Christ calls us to be and do. Successful churches, like successful people, can be affected by sins like pride and self-satisfaction – attitudes which are deeply challenged by Jesus in the gospels.

No matter how small the congregation, there can be new hope and new growth through turning afresh to God in faith, hope and love. Even two or three people gathered together to look at our Christian life as stewards of the resources God has entrusted us with, can be blessed with love, faith and vision. It can truly be a case of 'where two or three meet together in my name, I am there among them' (Matthew 18).

It may well begin with a focus on money, for experience shows that a congregation whose members give generously has many marks of spiritual vitality, supportive fellowship, outgoing witness and growth in it.

Stewards

A steward is someone who has been entrusted with the care of someone else's property, like a farm, a household, or some money. The steward will at some time have to account to the owner for how that property has been looked after.

The idea of stewardship is of great concern today throughout the world as many people have become very conscious of how prodigal we have been with the earth's resources, particularly in the last two centuries.

We have rather arrogantly believed we could exploit chemicals and fossil fuels, could alter the ecology by dams, drainage, and deforestation, and pour our waste products into rivers and seas without too great a concern for the consequences of so doing. Now we have been brought to realize that we have to exercise careful stewardship of the earth's resources if we are not to make it impossible for life to continue, or to have any worthwhile quality for future generations of our children and grandchildren.

This, it seems to me, is one of the factors that have prodded us Christians to re-examine the full meaning of Christian stewardship. It is not a narrow focus simply on financing the church. It is realizing the whole spectrum of our glad and grateful response to God for all the blessings of creation, for all that Christ has done for us, and all the gifts that the Holy Spirit of God has given us.

Christian stewardship now

The report *Christian Stewardship in the 1980s*,[1] published by the British Council of Churches in March 1980, set a definition of Christian stewardship as:

'The response which the Church and men and women are called to make to God for all that he has given to us and done for us, above all in Jesus Christ.

'In this response

- we worship God with praise and thankfulness;
- we look on the universe as God's creation;
- we treat the earth and its resources as God's provision for the needs of all mankind;
- we regard our lives, our powers, and our possessions as gifts from God to be enjoyed and used in his service;
- we seek to be stewards of the gospel and to share in Christ's mission to the world.'

This picks up the thread of King David's prayer when he offered to God the materials, money, and skills of his people for building the first Temple in Jerusalem. Those words, in the first book of Chronicles, chapter 29, are used each week in most Church of England churches as the prayer when the money, bread, wine, and water for the communion, representing the labour and joys of our daily life, are offered at the altar.

> Yours, Lord, is the greatness, the power,
> the glory, the splendour, and the majesty;
> for everything in heaven and on earth is yours.
> All things come from you,
> and of your own do we give you.

This important sense of God's generosity to us, and that our giving to him is simply offering him what is his in the first place, that his will may be done on earth as it is in heaven, is at the heart of current thinking about Christian stewardship. It is from this great prayer, which spans three thousand years of worship, giving, and stewardship of God's gifts, that we get the title of this book: *Yours, Lord*.

Christian stewardship and world problems

That 1980 statement from the British Council of Churches went on to suggest that the principle of Christian stewardship is important if there is to be a responsible attitude by rich and poor nations alike to the world's natural resources.

'Unless these problems are dealt with by the nations with wisdom and co-operation, they will produce economic recession and unemployment even in the rich nations of the world, and in poor countries they will aggravate situations where millions already go short of the essentials of life and population is increasing.' Those forecasts of 1980 are painfully accurate for many people in this and other countries in the 1990s.

'To deal with these problems more will be required than wise political decisions and economic policies . . . modern industrial society is involved in some kind of crisis which manifests itself in inflation, various types of unrest, rising crime rates, drug addiction, and so on.

'What is being called into question, so it seems, is not our technical competence, but our value system and the very aims and objects we are pursuing.'

Some scientists have argued that changes which are necessary to prevent global catastrophe are possible only 'if fundamental changes in the values and attitudes occur, such as a new ethic and a new attitude towards nature'. Values and attitudes are exactly what we are concerned with in Christian stewardship.

The Churches and Christian stewardship

The document goes on to spell out the danger that Churches will be tempted to concentrate on their own needs and problems, rather than the needs of the world for the message with which the Church has been entrusted.

'It is imperative that Christian stewardship should be presented and practised, not merely as a means of extricating the Churches from their financial problems, but as a total response to God . . . and as a means of advancing the mission of Christ in the world.'

This is a theme taken up by, amongst others, the Church of England report *Receiving and Giving*,[2] the Methodist Church report and study programme *Buried Treasure*,[3] and the Church of Scotland's *Christian Stewardship Manual*.[4]

Christian stewardship and mission

This mission of Christ in the world:

- relates our obedience to God the Creator with how we use his creation;
- relates our worship of God in church with how we seek to serve God in our everyday life;
- relates our love for God with our love for our neighbour.

We are invited to ask ourselves very searching questions about whether our time, money and energy is too much bound up in maintaining our church buildings where they are and as they are now. Jesus commanded his disciples to go out to convey his good news to people in the world. Do we run the risk of putting our emphasis too much on inviting them to come into his house to hear it?

Where Christians have an inner conviction of the importance of the good news of Christ, and are eager to help others discover the 'pearl of great price' that we have found, there is a willingness to use our money, our energies, and our buildings more generously and imaginatively in God's service.

Christian Stewardship in the 1980s also calls us to review how we seek to share our good news with our neighbours in Britain, and to learn from our fellow Christians in other countries. A large number of them belong to Churches which were established by Christians from Britain.

Many of these Churches now have large congregations, are growing fast, and are spiritually strong. We can learn much from them, if we have enough love, humility and willingness to do so. We can learn particularly the value of recognizing and using the gifts of all our members.

Every member a minister

Every baptized Christian is a minister of the gospel. Saint Paul in Romans chapter 12, and 1 Corinthians 12, compares the Church to a human body, in which every limb and organ has its proper function. The body is only working as it is intended to when every one of its members is doing its part. The ministry of the Church should be the ministry of all its members.

But at the same time, our service to God is not just in church or on church business. We serve God at work, in our home and family life, in our involvement with voluntary service, in local government, politics, unions and business organizations. We can serve God by the behaviour we show and the views we explain in social gatherings and in our leisure pursuits. There is no part of life which is not God's.

To do this well all of us need training. Both ordained and lay members are encouraged in that Report to set a high priority on training to be even more effective in understanding and practising our Christian faith in our everyday life and work.

Money matters

All these important aspects of Christian stewardship have been mentioned before we come to the matter of money. Perhaps because, as I noted before, it's a touchy subject with church members. The Report states:

'Although church members recognize the need for money to provide for government, business and the life of the home, they do not frankly recognize the Church's need for money to maintain its life and work.'

It goes on to tick off the clergy and other leaders for being shy about talking of money to church members.

'Although leaders of congregations know their congregation's need for greater giving, many are reluctant to visit members and speak to them personally about giving . . . Although teaching on the use of money and possessions is given throughout the Bible, many ministers do not give this teaching its due place and emphasis in their preaching and teaching.

'These mistaken views have serious consequences. They prevent members from fulfilling their commitment as Christians. They keep leaders of congregations and church committees engrossed in dealing with problems of finance. They hinder the Churches from taking part effectively in Christ's mission.'

Generosity

While it does not mention that many churches have been revitalized in their whole life and mission through a programme in which their members were invited radically to review their levels of financial giving, it does give us a bird's eye view of the biblical teaching about money, possessions, and giving, in the context of Christian life and prayer.

It is emphasized again and again throughout the Bible that such financial giving is a tangible expression of our faith, our gratitude, and our commitment to God. Generous giving is always associated with receiving blessing. Paul wrote to the church at Corinth (2 Corinthians 8 and 9) to encourage them to be generous in giving money to help their fellow Christians in Jerusalem: Greek Christians to give generously to support Jewish Christians.

'You are so rich in everything – in faith, speech, knowledge, and diligence of every kind, as well as in the love you have for use – that you should surely show yourselves equally lavish in this generous service! This is not meant as an order; by telling you how keen others are I am putting your love to the test.

'You know the generosity of our Lord Jesus Christ: he was rich, yet for your sake he became poor, so that through his poverty you might become rich . . . If we give eagerly according to our means, that is acceptable to God; he does not ask for what we do not have.

'Remember: sow sparingly, and you will reap sparingly; sow bountifully, and you will reap bountifully. Each person should give as he has decided for himself; there should be no reluctance, no sense of compulsion; God loves a cheerful giver. And it is in God's power to provide you with all good gifts in abundance, so that, with every need always met to the full, you may have something to spare for every good cause; as scripture says: "He lavishes his gifts on the needy; his benevolence lasts for ever." '

Faith and finance

The British Council of Churches Report points out that the writers of the Bible, and Jesus himself, make it clear that 'our response to God, our commitment to Christ, our love for our neighbour, and our own spiritual state are all intimately linked with our attitude to money and our possessions, and the use which we make of them'. Faith and finance are linked closely together.

'It was through the giving of money and material things that Zaccheus expressed his repentance; the good Samaritan showed love for his neighbour; and those who were kind to one of the least of their brethren served their Lord and entered his Kingdom.'

On the other hand, 'It was through their greed for money and possessions that men made God's Temple a "den of robbers"; the prodigal son made a ruin of his life; and a rich man failed to show kindness to a poor man at his gate'.

An attitude to all our money dealings

'The biblical teaching about money applies to our total dealing with money – to the way we regard money, the way we earn money, and the way we use money. This teaching is particularly relevant in a society which is predominantly materialistic.

'In such a society, Christians are called to take a stand against the pressure of prevailing opinion and the temptation to greed, to provide honestly and moderately for their own needs, and to give for the needs of others.

'Giving an offering for the work of the Church must have high priority for Christians. This is not simply because much of the work of the Church depends on members' giving, but primarily because our offering expresses our faith in God, our commitment to Christ, and our concern for the advancement of his work in the world.

'Our offering should therefore be based on a personal decision about the proportion of our income which we will give to express our commitment and concern.'

This brings us back to the four aspects of Christian stewardship outlined in the Report.

Christian stewardship is:

• thankfulness and praise to God for the whole of his creation;

- to regard the resources of the earth as riches to be used responsibly to benefit all mankind;
- to regard our lives, our powers, and our possessions as gifts from God to be enjoyed and used in his service;
- to be responsible for sharing in Christ's mission to the world, helping others to come to Christ, and together with us, sharing in the work of Christ today.

It is essentially making a whole-hearted commitment to our God in every part of our life.

This is very different from the stereotype image of Christian stewardship as a way of making sure the church can pay its way. It is a description of the elements of a lively faith, rather than one which is merely alive.

A lively faith

I remember hearing of a Yorkshire churchwarden who disliked the change of wording in the revised communion service in 1928 from 'lively faith' to 'living faith'. As he pointed out: 'Look at our Vicar. He's living, but he ain't lively.'

If our own experience of the Christian life, both in our own personal contact with God, and in the life of the church to which we belong, is not very enriching, there is something very positive we can do about it.

A group of people, no matter how small the group is, can take the initiative to read about, think about, pray about, and then plan to act on our understanding of Christian stewardship. This will affect, challenge, and enrich our own lives, and that of the church to which we belong.

So let's explore this further, realizing that it offers ideas that are likely to lead to changes in our thinking, our values, our relationships, and our behaviour. These in turn can lead to changes in the worship, fellowship, teaching, service and mission of the congregation to which we belong.

The initiative is likely to come from the clergy, but it doesn't have to. Lay members can take initiatives too. What matters is that any church member who is encouraged by the ideas in this book, and the practical suggestions for acting upon them, should take some steps to share this thinking with fellow members of their church.

References

1   *Christian Stewardship in the 1980s* (Church in Wales Publications, Woodland Place, Penarth CF6 2EX).

2   *Receiving and Giving: The Basis, Issues and Implications of Christian Stewardship*, General Synod of the Church of England, GS 943 (1990).

3   *Buried Treasure – An Exploration into Christian Giving*, Brian Brown (Methodist Publishing House, undated; ISBN 0-946550-63-8).

4   *Christian Stewardship Manual*, The Board of Stewardship and Finance of the Church of Scotland (St Andrew Press, 1991).

2

Stewardship not Ownership

There are important teachings in the Bible which challenge some of the attitudes to money, property, and stewardship which we commonly accept today.

The biblical principle is that all land belongs to God. So the Old Testament law insisted that if a landowner had to mortgage or sell his land, he could not be deprived of it permanently. It would be returned to him in the Jubilee Year, which was every 50 years.

The beliefs on which our property market is based today are very different from this. Many people who were able to afford to buy their houses before interest rates rose have now fallen behind in their payments, and lost both their home and their savings.

Rescue packages have been introduced so that some people can be credited with the proportion of the house they have paid for, and become tenants of a Housing Association for the remainder. This is a way of enabling the family to stay together in their home.

It makes social, ethical and economic sense. The sad thing is that it is a new development, introduced only in 1992 after political pressure, when so many homeowners were suffering from the combined effects of high interest rates and the recession, and to date has benefited only a few households.

Attitude adjusters

While the attitude of building societies and banks to mortgage defaulters has been to seek a repossession order as a normal routine, people have been turned out on the street. Many ended up in bed and breakfast accommodation, paid for by their local council. Often that cost more than their mortgage payments.

11

If the money lenders could be persuaded to change their attitudes, life could become less harsh and unfair for those who could benefit from this. It is important to note that there is no system of dealing with money that cannot change if the will is there to do things differently.

Decisions are powered by beliefs: attitudes can be adjusted. Christian stewardship is very much about challenging and changing current ethics and attitudes to ownership of goods, property, and land.

Beliefs and attitudes change

Convictions and attitudes about money play a big part in our lives. We tend to assume that the money system operates in the way it does because it is obvious and practical, and that there is no alternative.

But attitudes to debt have changed considerably in the last 150 years, as you can see in Dickens's novel *Little Dorrit*. Debtors then who could not repay what they owed went to prison. They stayed there until the debt was repaid.

Things have changed even more in the past 2,000 years, for Jesus' story of the two debtors (Luke 7) gives us the horrifying prospect for debtors in his time of themselves and their families, and all their property, being sold to pay their debt.

We no longer sell debtors into slavery, and those people who do go to prison for debt now know how long they have to serve there. We accept that there are other ways of dealing with issues of money and property. The way we choose depends upon our values and beliefs.

It is only in recent times that the law in England and Wales has recognized that a married woman has a right to an equal share in her husband's assets, even if everything is legally in his name alone, and not in joint names.

In the last century, when a woman married, all her property became her husband's, and in fact she too was regarded as his property. Married women are now partners, not property, because attitudes, values and beliefs have changed.

Attitudes to services

Whilst we in Britain are used to receiving medical treatment on the National Health Service, in America people can be asked what medical insurance they have, before an ambulance will take them to hospital. They may be unable to get treatment if they cannot pay for it. Chronic illness can use up all their medical insurance cover. They may well have to use their savings, sell their goods and even their home, to pay for long-term medical care.

We are beginning to experience a touch of this as families have to pay topping-up fees for private nursing care for dependent elderly people. Some residents fear being evicted from their nursing home if neither they nor their family can contribute to the cost of their care.

Students, and others on low incomes, may not now be able to afford a sight test, or dental treatment, because they cannot pay the charges. The decision to charge for dental treatment, sight tests, and medical or nursing treatment stems from a particular set of beliefs and attitudes.

Ethical issues

Whatever view we take of how to regard and use money, the issues that we are dealing with are ethical ones – choices of what is appropriate. The economist J. M. Keynes wrote: 'There are practically no issues of policy, as distinct from technique, which do not involve ethical considerations.'[1] He is making the same point that the British Council of Churches Report made on Christian stewardship and world poblems.

So, if policy options and decisions in matters of finance involve ethical considerations, we need to examine the basis for our Christian values, attitudes, and beliefs about our stewardship of money, property, and possessions, and indeed of the whole of our life.

These come from four main sources in the scriptures: the sacred law of the Hebrew people, the Torah; the teachings of their prophets; the teaching of Jesus; and the teaching and experience of the Church in New Testament times. We look in this chapter at the Old Testament view of stewardship.

A Hebrew view

In the Hebrew scriptures, men and women are presented as stewards of God's abundant creation. The beauty, the complexity and the immensity of this created world is described in Job 37 to 41 and Ecclesiasticus 43.

The human beings whom God created in his own image, male and female, are entrusted with the stewardship of the multitude of plant, animal, bird, fish and insect life, as well as the mineral

resources. They are accountable to God for them (Genesis 1 and 2).
This is the basis of our concept of Christian stewardship.

The Promised Land

When Moses was sent by God to bring his people out of slavery in
Egypt, he was told to lead them to the land God had promised to
Abraham and his descendants, 'a land flowing with milk and
honey'.

Gratitude to God is the keynote of all that Moses teaches his
people. It begins with the song of thanksgiving they sang when they
had safely crossed the sea and escaped from the pursuing Egyptians
(Exodus 15).

The Old Testament is threaded through with the notion that God
cares tenderly for his wayward people, providing them with protection and victory, food and drink, and a land richly endowed
(Deuteronomy 8).

It is a land where they will never suffer scarcity. They are
reminded: 'When you have plenty to eat, bless the Lord your God
for the good land he has given you. See that you do not forget the
Lord your God by failing to keep his commandments.'

And when they enjoy all these things, they are to remember who
gave them these benefits. They must guard against the dangers of
thinking: ' "My own strength and energy have gained me with
wealth". Remember the Lord your God; it is he who gives you
strength to become prosperous' (Deuteronomy 8).

Thanksgiving

This theme of thanksgiving is important to us Christians too. It is a
key element in our worship, especially the Eucharist – our thanksgiving to God for all that he has given us and done for us. It is at the
root of the Christian understanding of the stewardship of all our
resources, recognizing that we have received them from God,
expressing our gratitude to him, and handling them as resources
entrusted to us by God.

Thanksgiving and faithfulness to God are seen as two sides of the
same coin in Deuteronomy 11 and 12.

While God asks his people to make material sacrifices, to move to
unknown destinations, to endure considerable hardship in the process, he also promises them great blessings. He is not challenging
them to live a life of poverty: he is challenging them to live a life of
obedience and gratitude in which they will be greatly blessed.

They have to be willing to sacrifice things that stand in the way of them being adaptable, adventurous, and faithful to God's great purpose for them.

It is the same for us Christians today. We are promised great blessings – and we too are challenged by God to be grateful and faithful, willing to sacrifice traditions, structures, and forms of worship or organization that prevent us from being faithful to God's will and vision for us in changing circumstances.

Celebrations and tithes

Life for the Hebrews was not all self-sacrifice and suffering. They had great parties and celebrations. They were to come together in a combined act of worship and thanksgiving.

They were to bring 'whole-offerings and sacrifices, your tithes and contributions, and all the choice gifts that you have vowed to the Lord. You will rejoice in the presence of the Lord your God' with families, servants, and the priests (Deuteronomy 14).

They were also to set aside a tenth of all their produce. This was to be offered in thanksgiving to God, and to provide the food for a great celebration feast, for themselves and the Levites (the priests who had no ancestral land) in the presence of God. This was not so much a duty as a joy: it was gratitude money. The giving was to be an act of celebration, revelling in all their blessings, and in giving the tenth, honouring the source of all their wealth: God.

Lending and giving

They were not to charge interest on money they lent to fellow countrymen. They might do so to foreigners, but not to their own (Exodus 22 and Deuteronomy 23).

At the end of every seventh year, the lenders had to renounce all claims on money they had lent to fellow countrymen. They might press foreigners for repayment, but not their own people (Deuteronomy 15).

They were promised that there would never be any poor among them if only they would obey God's commandments. If any of their people became poor 'do not be hard-hearted or close-fisted towards him in his need. Be open-handed towards him and lend him on pledge as much as he needs.'

Furthermore, 'Should a fellow-Hebrew, be it a man or a woman, sell himself to you as a slave, he is to serve you for six years. In the seventh year you must set him free, and when you set him free, do not let him go empty-handed. Give him lavishly from your flock, from your threshing-floor and your winepress. Be generous to him, as the Lord your God has blessed you . . . Bear in mind that you were slaves in Egypt and the Lord your God redeemed you.'

This is an astonishing programme of stewardship behaviour. It is a theological attitude which challenges the ethics and attitudes of our modern labour, money, and property markets.

And there is more. Social responsibility is part of the Hebrew concept of stewardship of the land and its produce, expressed in giving and receiving, generosity and compassion, and in personal relationships.

Land and Jubilees

Every 50 years the Israelites had to hold a Jubilee Year, when all the land that had been sold had to be returned to its original owner. God's directive was that 'no land may be sold outright, because the land is mine, and you come to it as aliens and tenants of mine' (Deuteronomy 25). The key to this is in verse 17: 'You must not victimize one another, but fear your God.' The attitude to property and wealth was based on the conviction that it all belonged to God, and his people must care for one another with compassion and fairness.

It is a great ideal, but sadly not one that seems to have been practised for very long in Israel. However, the principle is sound. William Temple commended the idea that 'we must recover reverence for the earth and its resources, treating it no longer as a reservoir of potential wealth to be exploited, but as a storehouse of divine bounty on which we utterly depend'.[2]

Christian stewardship

Giving gratefully and joyfully in thanksgiving to God for our material prosperity is an important aspect of Christian stewardship that comes from the time of the earliest encounters of God with his chosen people.

Closely linked with it is a social compassion and responsibility for people who are in need. The prime concern is to care for people before profits.

The Hebrew idea, that we are stewards of God's earth, contrasts with the idea that owners can do what they like with their own property.

It would be stretching it too far to identify any modern concept of ecological stewardship in their thinking, but the insistence that farmers left some corn in their fields for poor people to pick, rather than extract the very last grain for themselves, sets a style of responsible use of the earth's resources, and a willingness to share prosperity with those whose lives depend upon us sitting lightly to our possessions (Deuteronomy 24: 17–end, and Ruth 2).

This attitude is one that Jesus strongly emphasized in his life and teaching, as we shall see in the next chapter.

References

1   *Christianity and Social Order*, William Temple (SPCK, 1976), from the Introduction by Ronald Preston, p. 9.
2   *Ibid.*, p. 111.

3

Jesus' Approach to Stewardship

I vividly remember, even after 30 years, the emotional turmoil I experienced over a small pair of candle-holders. Their cash value was trivial: their emotional value to me was considerable.

I lent them to our church for a special occasion. Afterwards the Rector said they looked so good there he was sure I would want to give them to the church. I did, but not gladly. I felt I had been spiritually blackmailed.

I had used the candle-holders for some years at home, often lighting a candle when I prayed at the end of a day. Parting with them was painful. I was angry.

What I slowly came to realize was the hold that such possessions had on my mind and emotions, and how that hold could interfere with my relationships with God and with other people, and how it disturbed my inner self.

Trivial as the subject of that incident was, it helped me to experience the significance of what Jesus said about the choice between God and possessions. We can either put our relationship with God first, or we can put our possessions first. We cannot do both at the same time: 'You cannot serve God and money' (Luke 16.13). This is a key principle of *Christian* stewardship.

Sit lightly to possessions

When a fellow in a crowd wanted Jesus to get his brother to divide the family property with him, he got more than he bargained for. Jesus told him to sit lightly to possessions: 'Be on your guard against greed of every kind', Jesus said, and warned of the

18

dangerous consequences for a person 'who piles up treasure for himself and remains a pauper in the sight of God'.

Then Jesus goes on to tell his disciples not to be preoccupied with concerns about food, clothing, and long life: 'Your Father knows that you need them. No, set your minds on his kingdom, and the rest will come to you as well . . . For where your treasure is, there will your heart be also.' This too is a key aspect of *Christian* stewardship.

He follows this up with instructions always to be ready, and illustrates it with the parable of the steward in charge of his master's property (Luke 12). Our stewardship is exercised in our conscientious care of our master's property.

Jesus doesn't tell us to live without material comforts; he simply says don't make them your god. Be content to live simply, and in your life and work be close to God: that is a stewardship that is richly blessed by God. For 'What does anyone gain by winning the whole world at the cost of destroying himself?' (Luke 9.25).

The importance of relationships

We are called to exercise Christian stewardship in our relationships with other people, and not be so preoccupied with material things that we lose our sense of justice and compassion.

Jesus illustrates this in his story of the two people who owed money. One who owed an enormous sum was due to be sold, along with his wife and family and possessions. He pleaded for time to pay, and had the debt cancelled. He immediately went and collared a chap who owed him a sum tiny in comparison, and had him imprisoned for debt (Matthew 18).

A man came to Jesus asking what he must do to win eternal life. Jesus quotes the last six of the Ten Commandments, which the fellow says he has observed since he was a boy. 'As Jesus looked at him, his heart warmed to him.

' "One thing you lack" he said. "Go, sell everything you have, and give to the poor, and you will have treasure in heaven; then come and follow me." At these words his face fell and he went away with a heavy heart; for he was a man of great wealth.' He hadn't expected anything so drastic.

This man's attachment to his wealth meant more to him than anything else: it stood in the way of his relationship with God.

Hard for the wealthy

'Jesus looked round at his disciples and said to them, "How hard it will be for the wealthy to enter the kingdom of God!" Then he joked, "It is easier for a camel to pass through the eye of a needle than for a rich man to enter the kingdom of God." '

He sums up the essence of what God asks of us: 'You must love the Lord your God with all your heart, with all your soul, with all your mind, and with all your strength', and 'you must love your neighbour as yourself'. This too is one of the key themes of Christian stewardship.

While he makes great demands on those who will follow him, he also makes it clear that a sacrifice gladly made for the sake of him and the gospel will be amply rewarded with his blessings.

'Anyone who wants to be a follower of mine must renounce self; he must take up his cross and follow me' he told his disciples. 'Whoever wants to save his life will lose it, but whoever loses his life for my sake and the gospel's will save it' (Mark 10).

Generosity not legalism

Jesus' approach to generosity was something quite startling. He told a story of a farmer who hired day labourers at different times during the day. They all agreed to the day's wage when they started. At the end of the day, they all received a full day's pay. Those who had worked all day felt they were entitled to some extra.

The farmer turned to one of them and said, 'My friend, I am not being unfair to you. You agreed on the usual wage for the day, did you not? Take your pay and go home. I choose to give the last man the same as you. Surely I am free to do what I like with my own money? Why be jealous because I am generous?' (Matthew 20).

In the same way Jesus admired not the rich people dropping their gifts into the Temple treasury, but the poor widow who put in two tiny coins. ' "I tell you this" he said: "this poor widow has given more than any of them; for those others who have given had more than enough, but she, with less than enough, has given all she had to live on" ' (Luke 21).

Generosity is a lovely attribute, and we only practise it when relationships are more important to us than our possessions. It is easy to be generous to our nearest and dearest relatives and friends: Christian stewardship calls us to exercise a generous spirit to those from whom we cannot expect to receive anything in return, not even affection or gratitude (Luke 6).

Unlimited goodness

Jesus encourages us to be generous in all ways, not just financially. He did not approve of the tit-for-tat mentality of response or giving. Instead of the eye-for-an-eye and tooth-for-a-tooth attitude, he said, 'But what I tell you is this: Do not resist those who wrong you. If anyone slaps you on the right cheek, turn and offer him the other also.

'If anyone wants to sue you and take your shirt, let him have your cloak as well. If someone in authority presses you into service for one mile, go with him two.

'Love your enemies and pray for your persecutors; only so can you be children of your heavenly Father, who causes the sun to rise on good and bad alike . . . If you love only those who love you, what reward can you expect? Even the tax collectors do as much as that.

'If you greet only your brothers, what is there extraordinary about that? Even the heathen do as much. There must be no limit to your goodness, as your heavenly Father's goodness knows no bounds' (Matthew 5).

Accounting for our behaviour

Jesus presents a powerful warning to any of us who think that being ungenerous to others is something which we can choose to do or not, without any consequences. He told a story depicting God's approach to judgement, when we shall account for how we have behaved in this life. God is likened to a shepherd who separates the sheep from the goats. Those who inherit the kingdom are those who have demonstrated generosity in their lives: those who haven't get short shrift.

He illustrates this with examples of those who gave food to hungry people, a drink to thirsty people, hospitality to strangers, provided clothes for those who had none, gave help to people who were ill, and visited people in prison. 'Anything you did for one of my brothers here, however insignificant, you did for me' said Christ (Matthew 25).

Christian stewardship is the very opposite behaviour to that of the ostentatious scribes 'who eat up the property of widows, while for appearance's sake they say long prayers' (Mark 12.40).

On the other hand, he had special praise for the stewardship of the woman at Bethany who anointed him with very costly perfume. The disciples were indignant and complained about the waste, saying that its value could have been given to the poor. Jesus recognized and valued her way of being generous, in preparation for his impending burial (Matthew 26).

Attitudes rather than rules

Jesus always urged an attitude of sitting lightly to possessions, loyalty to God, and being open-hearted and open-handed to people in need.

He criticized the religious establishment of his day for being concerned about the minute details of the rules and regulations of their law, whilst neglecting the attitudes and actions those obligations were intended to express.

The Pharisees, conscientious people who didn't want to put a foot wrong in their religious observances, were meticulous about paying their tithes and showing off about the amounts of money they gave in the Temple. It cut no ice with Jesus because it was all self-centred, rather than God-centred. It was all show and no substance: 'they say one thing and do another' (Matthew 23).

He ridiculed them for the contrast between the care with which they gave a tenth of everything, even of their garden herbs, 'but neglect justice and the love of God. It is these you should have practised, without overlooking the others' he told them (Luke 11.42).

Tithing

There are some Christians who believe that as the Hebrew law prescribes tithing, as well as various other thank-offerings and gift-offerings, the tithe should be the least a Christian should be giving to God's work. That is a minimum of ten per cent of our income, given to enable the work of the Church and to other Christian and humanitarian concerns.

Jesus mentions the tithe only three times in all, and each time he is critical of the way it is being observed (Matthew 23.23; Luke 11.42; 18.12). Nowhere else in the New Testament are tithes mentioned, except in Hebrews, chapter 7.

What he appears to be criticizing is the idea that paying the money without necessarily living the godly life is what God wants. Christian stewardship keeps generosity of pocket together with generosity of love and faithfulness. Jesus' concern is with the underlying purpose of the tithes (Deuteronomy 14).

The invitation and the challenge

Jesus taught the importance of good stewardship of the whole of our life. We are answerable to God for how we live, the priorities, values and choices we make, for our attitudes, and for how we use our money and possessions.

This is true for each one of us individually, and for us corporately as a congregation, a diocesan or district fellowship, as a Christian Communion and as citizens not only of our own nation but of the world.

Christian stewardship is exercised in trying to put into practice Jesus' teaching and attitudes: generosity of care, relationships, money, and possessions. His teaching is the base line for our whole attitude to life, which is what we are seeking to look at afresh in this book.

4

Prophets, Profits and People

Centuries before Christ, the prophets had taught that loyalty to God required faithfulness in relationships and generosity in religious offerings and celebrations.

All too often the people performed routine rituals without engaging the heart, mind and will: they sang praises to God in the Temple but practised evil in their everyday lives. This was not godly stewardship.

Jesus echoed the prophets' teaching. He is twice recorded quoting approvingly from the prophet Hosea (Matthew 9.13; 12.7): 'For I require loyalty, not sacrifice, acknowledgement of God rather than whole-offerings' (Hosea 6.6).

The opening salvo from the prophecies of Isaiah of Jerusalem take up the same theme:

'Your countless sacrifices, what are they to me? says the Lord. I am sated with whole-offerings . . . the reek of sacrifice is abhorrent to me . . . your festivals; they have become a burden to me . . . Though you offer countless prayers, I shall not listen . . . cease to do evil, learn to do good. Pursue justice, guide the oppressed; uphold the rights of the fatherless, and plead the widow's cause' (Isaiah 1.11–17).

Change your ways

Earlier, Amos, a sheep farmer from Tekoa, had been sent to declare to the people that the way they were regularly behaving was entirely the opposite of God's way: selling their own folk into slavery, being arrogantly class-conscious and debauched.

'They sell honest folk for silver, and the poor for a pair of sandals. They grind the heads of the helpless into the dust and push the humble out of their way. Father and son resort to the temple girls, so profaning my holy name. Men lie down beside every altar on garments held in pledge, and in the house of their God they drink wine on the proceeds of fines' (Amos 2.6–8).

He describes the businessmen 'giving short measure in the bushel and taking overweight in the silver, tilting the scales fraudulently, and selling the refuse of the wheat' (Amos 8.5, 16).

God required very different behaviour: 'I take no pleasure in your sacred ceremonies . . . Spare me the sound of your songs . . . Instead let justice flow on like a river and righteousness like a never-failing torrent' (Amos 5.21–24).

The same concerns were later expressed by Micah: 'The Lord has told you mortals what is good, and what it is that the Lord requires of you: only to act justly, to love loyalty, to walk humbly with your God' (Micah 6.8). These are words that inspire much of our understanding of Christian stewardship.

Repentance

Through the prophets God invites his people to come back to him; if they repent and reform, he is always ready to forgive them, and to start afresh with renewed blessings on them.

'Yet even now, says the Lord, turn back to me wholeheartedly with fasting, weeping and mourning. Rend your hearts and not your garments, and turn back to the Lord your God, for he is gracious and compassionate, long-suffering and ever constant, ready always to relent when he threatens disaster' (Joel 2.12, 13).

He admonishes them as naughty children: 'I, the Lord do not change, and you have not ceased to be children of Jacob. Ever since the days of your forefathers you have been wayward and have not kept my laws. If you return to me, I shall turn back to you.' This invitation to repentance is still at the heart of our concern to review our own stewardship of the gospel with which we have been entrusted.

On this occasion they stand accused of having defrauded God in the tithes. So his offer of forgiveness invites them to: 'Bring the whole tithe into the treasury; let there be food in my house. Put me to the proof, says the Lord of Hosts, and see if I do not open windows in the sky and pour a blessing on you as long as there is need' (Malachi 3.6–10).

Stewardship of the whole of life

What we have in these quotations is a series of calls to practise godly stewardship in every aspect of life: money, possessions, honest trading, social relationships, treatment of vulnerable people, repentance, and due honour and gratitude to God. The stewardship of life has to be practised in the temple and the market place, in the home, on the farm, and in all business dealings. God calls people to change their lives.

Jesus criticized the Pharisees for doing variations of what the prophets had so vigorously condemned. One example is the oral tradition they practised which permitted a man to devote his possessions to God. That sounds on the face of it to be genuinely religious, an example of good stewardship, but they used it as a reason for refusing financial help to their elderly parents.

Jesus did not mince his words about this piece of religious jiggery pokery: 'You have made God's law null and void out of regard for your tradition. What hypocrites! How right Isaiah was when he prophesied about you: "This people pays me lip-service, but their heart is far from me; they worship me in vain, for they teach as doctrines the commandments of men" ' (Matthew 15.1-9).

Social stewardship

The vision of social responsibility and stewardship has prompted generations of Christians to fight against social evils such as slavery and child labour, to improve conditions of housing and employment for people who work in factories and mines, and conditions in prisons, mental hospitals, and orphanages.

The great concerns of Christian social reformers in the past are now appearing for us in a new guise. No longer in Britain do we have the child chimney sweeps and factory workers, but we still have exploitation and abuse of children.

Social services departments continually have to act to protect children who have been badly treated, and indeed some people have been convicted of abusing children they were employed to protect. Many people who knew for years of the children's complaints 'passed by on the other side' like the priest and the Levite in the parable of the Good Samaritan.

Many children and other vulnerable people in the community are, and many more could be, protected by Christian people of sensitivity, compassion, care and courage, who exercise their Christian stewardship in supporting, speaking and acting in their interests.

Some elderly people, mentally ill people, people with learning difficulties, and some people with physical disabilities, can be exploited or abused. So too can people with sensory impairment. The same can happen, and often does, to women, to older people, and people who live in an area that has a certain reputation.

It happens to people who have a different coloured skin, a different culture, or who speak a different language from most of the people in the area in which they live. That can apply to Welsh-speaking people in predominantly English-speaking areas, or English-speaking people in predominantly Welsh-speaking areas. It is more likely to happen to people whose first language is an Asian tongue.

Lepers and Lazarus

People who are badly disfigured, and people with particular illnesses like AIDS, can be treated by people in their local community to the same social ostracism as the lepers in the gospels.

Those of us, whether we are physically able or disabled, who become aware of that exploitation or abuse have a Christian duty to do something to help protect anyone who is vulnerable or in need. It requires of us the compassion, care and courage of the Good Samaritan.

It may involve us supporting the complaints of a blind man who falls over a bicycle lying on the pavement outside a shop door. It may involve us supporting women who are discriminated against in the jobs market, or resisting racial or sexual prejudice in private conversations.

Lazarus still sits at our gate, or sleeps rough in our cities. He may not ask for our help. Maybe no one else asks on his behalf. Just his presence places a big question mark over our understanding of our Christian stewardship of care for those whose needs the strong and powerful can ignore. Sometimes his place is round the corner out of sight, downtown; or else we see him on the television in our sitting room, filmed in distant countries.

Wherever there is an enormous gulf between our worship and

our behaviour, between what goes on in our church and what goes on in the homes, factories, shops, offices, meeting places and streets of our community, we have the same contrast between belief and behaviour that the Hebrew prophets were criticizing in their day, and Jesus criticized in his.

5

Lifestyle

I had high hopes when I became a Christian of belonging to a fellowship of like-minded people, with ideals and beliefs we would share, in an encouraging, warm and caring fellowship.

I get angry or hurt, and sometimes disappointed or sad, when I find that the motives, attitudes and actions of myself and of others fall very far short of our great ideals. Human frailty and sin are a fact of life we have to face.

Jesus contends with it by calling us to turn round, to face another way, and to follow him. He promises his Spirit will be with us always, and that we will be equipped with his Word, and be fed with the holy bread and wine of his life.

Even so, the history of Christian experience is that we regularly wander from that path. We lose our vision, and then we lose our way.

Loss of vision

If we lose that vision, what also dies is:

    our love for God,
    for our fellow members,
    for the people amongst whom we live and work.

Whenever Christians have behaved disgracefully, or their faith has grown dim or cold, or a comfortable worldliness has become more important than a lively faith in God, it is always the person of Christ in the gospels, with his profound spiritual values, who has challenged and inspired people to reach out for love, godliness, holiness, truth and beauty, and a life of simplicity. This is Christian stewardship.

The metaphor of the sower scattering his seed anywhere, so that some is squashed underfoot or gobbled up immediately, some choked in thistles, some rooted too shallowly for real growth, and yet others grow fruitfully, is still both vivid and apt 2,000 years later (Mark 4).

The year 2000

Very soon the whole world will be marking these 2,000 years of the Christian era. No doubt there will be parties, services and books galore for the occasion. An endless stream of radio and television programmes, articles in newspapers and magazines, plays and films will drench us in ideas, images and comments about it.

What will it all mean to you, to me, and to our fellow worshippers in church on Sunday? We may get a surfeit of comments on what effect Jesus of Nazareth has or has not had on civilization, spirituality, art, literature, architecture, law, society, and family life.

But the invitation and challenge of this dynamic person, whose freshness, originality and uniqueness leap out of the pages of St Mark's gospel, still stands for each of us: 'repent, and believe in the gospel'.

At the heart of the good news Jesus proclaims is the invitation to each person, and to each congregation, to commit ourselves afresh each day to him.

Follow me

Just as he challenged the man at the tax office (Mark 2) to 'follow me', so that challenge is implicit to each one of us to follow him in the choices, priorities, and values we make every day our lives.

As we prepare to celebrate the end of the second thousand years of the era of Christ we are challenged to examine what difference we allow Christ to make in our lifestyle. Is this Christ at the centre, or at the edge, of our life, both as individuals, and as a Christian congregation?

Stewardship of repentance

In the final book of the Bible, the Revelation of St John, is the letter that John, in his vision, is told to send to the Christians in Laodicea (end of chapter 3). The Laodiceans are challenged because they are lukewarm towards Christ: materially content, but spiritually blind.

This chastening rebuke could perhaps equally apply to many of us. Christ is seen by John to be saying that those he loves he reproves and chastens: 'Be wholehearted therefore in your repentance.'

We too need to consider the Christian stewardship of repentance. Wholeheartedness in loyalty to Christ, in love, faith and action, is the essence of Christian stewardship.

Christ knocks to come in

In John's vision Christ stands at the door and knocks. If anyone hears his voice and opens the door, Christ will enter. Christ knocks at our door, but doesn't barge into our lives. He waits with infinite patience for us to open the door when we are ready. Then begins a relationship which can change and enrich all others.

His good news challenges and inspires us, but does not force us, to share our lives with him. Those who respond to him wholeheartedly share a common life with him, a life whose characteristics are light, joy, and love. These are qualities which can shine even through suffering, pain and hardship. It is a life in which we are cleansed and forgiven.

The first letter of John sets all this out with a rich emphasis on love: God's great love for us, Christ's sacrificial love for us, and our love for God and for each other. 'Love must not be a matter of theory or talk; it must be true love which shows itself in action.'

A test of our commitment

A test of our commitment to Christ, and of our stewardship of his good news, is how we love our fellow Christians. 'This is what love really is: not that we have loved God, but that he loved us and sent his Son as a sacrifice to atone for our sins. If God thus loved us, my dear friends, we also must love one another . . . if we love one another, he himself dwells in us; his love is brought to perfection within us.'

It is this same task we, in our generation, are entrusted with. The 1990s are a time to examine how we are doing, and what sort of 2,000th birthday present we will be able to offer to Christ.

We recognize in ourselves, and in people around us, attitudes, values, ideals, and behaviour, which are very far from those that Christ invites us to adopt. We need to ask ourselves how effectively we apply our Christian beliefs, attitudes and actions in the decisions we make as leaders of our local church.

We cannot fail to be aware from television, radio and the

newspapers, that many twentieth-century people behave just as badly as many first-century people. The good news of the gospel is good news for us as much as it was for them.

Repent, and believe the gospel

Mark summarizes the theme of Jesus' message as: 'The time has arrived; the kingdom of God is upon you. Repent, and believe the gospel.' The word we translate as 'repent' has in the original more of a feel of turning round to face in a new direction. That is what we are invited to do.

We who have at one time or another made a conscious decision to have faith in Christ and his good news, recognize that we, and many of our fellow Christians, seem so often to have as little commitment and steadfastness as the disciples showed when Jesus needed them most.

Our worship may be faithfully and diligently conducted in our church, without making a real impact in changing us in the way Christ invites us to grow. It may make little difference to the quality of life in our neighbourhood. If that is so, it is poor stewardship, and we are back to the message of the prophets.

Resistance to change

It is not uncommon to find churches where there is a strong resistance by some members to any suggested change in the furnishing, pattern of life, and worship. We can become God's frozen people, more attached to what is familiar than to what might help the Christian mission be more effective.

It is possible to worship at a church regularly for years, be missing for a few months, and find that nobody has exercised a stewardship of care. No one has been in touch to see if we are all right.

It is also by no means uncommon to find churches where opportunities for growth and development in Christian living are stifled by jealous rivalries between people in positions of power and influence.

You get a very different feel of challenge, spiritual vitality, openness and freshness in the life and ministry of Jesus.

It contrasts with the conservative, protectionist, fearful and narrow perspectives that are characteristic of too much of our church life. God challenges us through the scriptures to review our concept of what it means to be wholehearted Christians, to be Christian stewards.

A different atmosphere

Where Christians are open to be led by the Holy Spirit, where there is a readiness to deepen our spiritual life, and where we celebrate with joy and thanksgiving, there is a different atmosphere and sense of direction in the church. People discover a lively faith where the worship is carefully prepared and presented.

Christians can feel encouraged and confident in a church where new ideas are not always considered a threat, but can be intelligently and sensitively appraised as a possible way forward. Christians can discover the reality of love in Christ where there is a deep and personal concern for every member, and for the world outside the church door.

Faith is not just exercised in prayer and practical care. It is also exercised, and can grow stronger, through developing our knowledge and understanding of our faith, and through reading, learning and participating in training. It is helped to grow when we commit ourselves to a particular discipline of Christian prayer and practice.

Attachments and barriers

This discipline includes our commitment to regular giving, both to the church and to those concerns which we feel contribute to our sense of Christian care and responsibility in society. We need to make a definite and considered decision about how much of our income we commit to God's work in his world, in gratitude and loyalty to him.

Like the man in St Mark's gospel, our attachment to our money can be a barrier to our attachment to God. So too can other attachments.

Those of us who became church members through an interest in caring service, church music, choir membership, flower arranging, fund raising, political action, soul culture, social contacts, or personal attachment to another person can be more attached to those aspects of church life than we are to Christ himself.

Comfort or discipline?

All of us at times can regard our Christian life principally as a source of personal comfort, guidance and spiritual treats. We then concentrate on meeting these needs, which are important and legitimate. The danger is that we can forget that we are also called to be disciplined, to take up our cross daily and follow Christ.

Whilst we are called to love God with all our heart, soul, mind and strength, we are also called to love our neighbours as we love ourselves. Christ and Paul suggest this includes a willingness to feed the hungry, visit the sick, rejoice with the happy, weep with the sorrowful, and introduce others to Christ.

Christ calls us to permeate the dough of society with the yeast of Christian life and love (Matthew 13.33). But his communication to us can be blocked by our greater attachment to other people, activities, things, or experiences.

We won't hear him at all if we expect only messages of comfort, and never expect him to challenge us, prod us, or discipline us towards more effective discipleship.

Life in all its fullness

John describes Jesus saying, 'I have come that they may have life, and may have it in all its fullness' (John 10.10). There are too many churches in which we have both sadly and painfully to recognize that 'life in all its fullness' is hardly an accurate description of the experience of those who attend it.

We are inclined to be very settled in the idea that religion is to comfort rather than challenge and stimulate us. We are inclined to see our religion as confirming our opinions, rather than enlarging our vision.

There is a great danger for us of complacency, of wanting religion to give us a feeling that our behaviour must be OK if we go to church regularly, rather than expecting our religion actually to change us, and to develop our practice of Christian love.

With a spiritual guide to help us understand what that might mean in practice, we can find a way to openness, freedom, fullness and simplicity. There are two books which I can happily commend as guides on this path to spiritual growth. They are written by Richard Foster, an American Quaker.

Celebration of Discipline

Celebration of Discipline[1] is a book that is easy to read, intensely practical and down to earth, which helps us also to soar to heaven. Richard Foster describes the spiritual disciplines as the 'door to liberation'.

He explains the Inward Disciplines of meditation, prayer, fasting, and study; the Outward Disciplines of simplicity, solitude, submission, and service; and the Corporate Disciplines of confession, worship, guidance, and celebration.

I think anyone who wants to understand, in a simple, modern and practical way, some of the key teachings of the classic spiritual writings of our faith, will find this book an attractive way into them, and one that makes a lot of sense.

Reading the Bible

Richard Foster recognizes that 'one of the great needs among Christians today is simply the reading of large portions of scripture. So much of our Bible reading is fragmented and sporadic.'

Most of our reading of scripture tends to be in short snatches for reading in church, or in some systematic method of reading a Bible passage each day. Even the readings in church are rarely given any introduction which might help us realize their background and context.

Reading the Bible can be both interesting and illuminating, especially if you have other books to help you. For example the Old Testament comes alive in a new way if you read it in tandem with a book like *The Living World of the Old Testament* by Bernhard W. Anderson.[2]

Stewardship of Christian education

I conducted a retreat in 1991 attended by 25 people from the church where I am a member. Most of them were aged over 55, and said the course of sermons and discussion groups in preparation for this was the first course of Christian education they had attended since they were confirmed more than 40 years before.

That is not too unusual these days, and it accounts for much loss of Christian vitality, confidence, commitment, and ability to articulate our faith.

We all need to exercise a Christian stewardship of study, to equip us to make more sense of our experiences of life, of our calling as Christians, and to know more thoroughly the way we seek to walk in. The art of making study interesting is something that Christian leaders, both clergy and lay, need to develop.

We can learn much from the experiential and distance-learning methods of modern adult education, and use this to enliven some of our traditional methods of Christian education and training.

Richard Foster invites us to learn by studying relationships between people, to study ourselves and our own natures, our inner feelings and mood swings, subjects we shall come to later in this book.

Simplicity

Every discipline has its corresponding freedom, says Foster. The Outward Discipline of solitude includes the freedom to be alone, to be still, to be able to see and hear more clearly even amidst the busyness of everyday life. It provides an opportunity for us to reorientate our life goals. Its fruit is increased sensitivity and compassion for others.

Foster explores the idea of simplicity much more fully in his second book, *Freedom of Simplicity*.[3] His theme here is that Christian simplicity frees us from the grip of the modern materialistic culture. It is very much a book about Christian stewardship in every aspect of our lives.

He offers guidance on the practicalities of living a life of Christian simplicity in the Western world at the end of this century.

The book is strong on exploring inner stillness, on real care for one another, on practical care of our environment, and of living generously and simply. It is a valuable means of helping us to consider how specific we will be about our Christian vision and lifestyle in the 1990s. That is no small achievement.

Foster offers us ways of beginning to practise outward simplicity, ways of sitting lightly to our possessions, as Jesus encouraged his hearers to do.

This seems a much harder thing to achieve in our acquisitive, consumer society, but Richard Foster offers us ways through: planned spending; exercising careful choice and discrimination in what we buy; how we invest our savings; how we may learn to give proportionately; to live frugally; and to give generously. These he commends as ways to liberation, the joy and freedom of simplicity.

He has things to say too about our influence in getting the Church and the world to take more seriously the importance of simplicity. It calls to mind a charity poster used some years ago: Live simply, that others may simply live.

Your money autobiography

Another way of exploring our approach to simplicity is to write a three-page money autobiography. It involves describing the role of money in your life from childhood to now. It is important to focus on feelings and relationships as well as the basic facts of what money you have had.

Money has quite a hold on all of us in different ways. If as a small group of Christians you each write your own money autobiography, and share it with each other, you may well find this an experience which deepens your self-understanding, and which can help you to grow spiritually.

Elizabeth O'Connor, in her book *Letter to Scattered Pilgrims*,[4] offers guidelines for this whole way of examining the role money plays in our life.

References

1   *Celebration of Discipline*, Richard Foster (Hodder & Stoughton, 1980).
2   *The Living World of the Old Testament*, Bernhard W. Anderson (Longman, 1971).
3   *Freedom of Simplicity*, Richard Foster (Triangle/SPCK, 1981).
4   *Letters to Scattered Pilgrims*, Elizabeth O'Connor (Harper and Row, San Francisco, 1979).

6

Being Practical, and Generous

The essence of good stewardship by Christians is to be both generous and practical in showing our love, gratitude, and concern for God, for his world, and his people – our God, our world, our people.

The New Testament letters are very realistic in applying Jesus' teaching. Paul, like Jesus, sat lightly to his possessions: 'I have learned to be self-sufficient whatever my circumstances. I know what it is to have nothing, and I know what it is to have plenty. I have been thoroughly initiated into fullness and hunger, plenty and poverty. I am able to face anything through him who gives me strength' (Philippians 4).

Paul, or more probably one of his close associates, was not unmindful of the very different needs of most Christians, as we see in the first letter to Timothy: 'If anyone does not make provision for his relations, and especially for members of his own household, he has denied the faith and is worse than an unbeliever.'

On the one hand people are to guard themselves against the harm that greed can do to them, and on the other hand they are to use their money constructively to co-operate with God in his care for those who need help.

Thus bishops must be above reproach, not avaricious, while deacons likewise must be dignified and not given to money-grubbing. Christians are to support widows and those in distress, 'in short, by doing good at every opportunity'.

Guarding against painful thorns

'Those who want to be rich fall into temptations and snares and into many foolish and harmful desires which plunge people into ruin

38

and destruction. The love of money is the root of all evil, and in pursuit of it some have wandered from the faith and spiked themselves on many a painful thorn.'

Debt counsellors, addicted gamblers, and those who have lost all their savings in speculative ventures, or just frittered away their money, know only too well the truth of this.

'But you, man of God, must shun all that, and pursue justice, piety, integrity, love, fortitude, and gentleness. Run the great race of faith and take hold of eternal life.'

'Instruct those who are rich in this world's goods not to be proud, and to fix their hopes not on so uncertain a thing as money, but on God, who richly provides all things for us to enjoy. They are to do good and to be rich in well doing, to be ready to give generously and to share with others, and so acquire a treasure which will form a good foundation for the future. Then they will grasp the life that is life indeed' (1 Timothy 5 and 6).

Giving generously, sharing with others, is not seen as a recipe to personal impoverishment, but as part of the way to eternal life. The good news of Jesus Christ is not about giving until it hurts, for the dubious pleasure of the masochistic pain it gives us. It is about enriching ourselves by being generous in giving to others.

Two visitors: one posh, one poor

James spells out the practical application of this generous behaviour in his letter: 'A pure and faultless religion in the sight of God the Father is this: to look after orphans and widows in trouble and to keep oneself untarnished by the world.'

He gives us a nice example of what he means, showing us that New Testament Christians were as prone to class (and racial?) consciousness in their churches as we are today.

'For instance', he writes, 'two visitors may enter your meeting, one a well-dressed man with gold rings, and the other a poor man in grimy clothes. Suppose you pay special attention to the well-dressed man and say to him, "Please take this seat", while to the poor man you say, "You stand over there, or sit here on the floor by my footstool", do you not see that you are discriminating among your members and judging by wrong standards?

'Listen, my dear friends: has not God chosen those who are poor in the eyes of the world to be rich in faith and to possess the kingdom he has promised to those who love him? And yet you have humiliated the poor man. Moreover, are not the rich your oppressors?'

'What good is it, my friends, for someone to say he has faith when his actions do nothing to show it? Can that faith save him? Suppose a fellow-Christian, whether man or woman, is in rags with not enough food for the day, and one of you says, "Goodbye, keep warm, and have a good meal", but does nothing to supply their bodily needs, what good is that? So with faith; if it does not lead to action, it is by itself a lifeless thing' (James 1 and 2).

Faith into action

We need therefore to consider very practical ways in which we can put our faith into action. We all benefit from having some sort of personal test of our own commitment.

Few are likely to imitate Levi, who left his job at the tax office and became a disciple of Jesus (Luke 5.27–39). Fewer still will feel the need to imitate Zaccheus, the rich superintendent of taxes, who, when he responded to Christ, gave half his considerable possessions to charity, and to anyone he had defrauded he offered to pay back 400 per cent! (Luke 19).

Some of our church leaders think their members can only be persuaded to give generously if they can see a financial crisis looming. They publicize target amounts, shares, and monthly financial records which show the difference between the church's expenditure and income each month.

This may be the practical stewardship of the bank balance, but it is not the invitation to that generosity of love, faith, and sitting lightly to possessions which Jesus, Paul and James speak of, and which we have come to recognize as Christian stewardship.

Financial commitment

Nothing is a clearer barometer of our commitment to Christ, our gratitude to God, our concern for people in need, than our readiness to be financially generous. A person who is committed in their pocket is very committed indeed.

Here I think we have to avoid two equally misleading approaches. One is to be so detailed in our guidelines that we fall into the trap many of the Hebrew people fell into. They thought that all that mattered was whether they had paid their tithes and offerings – irrespective of their behaviour in other aspects of their lives.

The other danger is to be so vague as to give no guidelines at all. 'Be generous', and leave it at that.

Problems of choosing a standard

Some Christians go back to the Torah and practise tithing. There are some for whom that may be right, but it is not for everyone. The danger is that tithers may be thought to be a cut above everyone else, which can breed spiritual arrogance. Or the tithe can be regarded as an upper limit, and so restrict those who wish to be more generous.

The tithe was the standard minimum payment for every Jew, rich and poor alike. They were required to give other offerings and alms besides. It was not paying their tithe that indicated their commitment to God, but how much they gave in alms.

There is also the view that tithing was part of the Hebrew state system, and most of us pay far more than a tithe in our taxes which provide for people who are in need of care, treatment and support. So, if we accept that we pay taxes as the Jewish people paid their tithes, let's see where generous proportionate giving in gratitude to God will take each of us in relation to our own net income.

Proportionate giving

I suggest we update the concept of proportionate giving enshrined in the idea of the tithe, and help ourselves and one another grow into a developing sense of commitment, generosity, faith and freedom.

Paul encouraged the Christians at Corinth, 'Every Sunday each of you is to put aside and keep by him whatever he can afford . . .' (1 Corinthians 16.2). So let us examine what we honestly feel we can afford to give in gratitude to God.

If we put that money aside, in a separate bank account or holding, we can then decide, quite separately, how we spend our 'Gratitude Money'. Some of it we will no doubt decide to give to our own local church, some to wider Christian concerns, and to individuals, causes, and organizations.

The motive for all our giving takes us back to the definition of Christian stewardship in the first chapter. This is to:

- express our gratitude to God;
- our commitment to Christ;
- to recognize our resources as part of God's provision for the needs of all mankind;
- to use our lives, powers and possessions as gifts from him to be used in his service; and
- to share in Christ's mission to the world.

What we need to do is to be really honest with ourselves about:

- what we can actually afford, and
- how much we feel we wish to commit ourselves to God in our lives.

If we test ourselves on both accounts proportionately, we will have a realistic means of deciding how much, and to whom, we will give our grateful giving. Paul encourages us to use our gifts in proportion to our faith (Romans 12.6), and this seems a helpful guideline for giving as well.

A person on a retirement income of about £80 a week (£320 a month) may prefer to work out their proportionate giving on a weekly basis. A person who earns near the national average wage perhaps gets a monthly payslip of about £800 net (£200 a week), and may prefer to work out their proportionate giving on a monthly basis.

Whichever basis we do it on, and whatever our income, it is not difficult to work out what 1 per cent or 10 per cent of our income is. Ten per cent of £80 is £8, and 1 per cent of £80 is 80 p, just as 10 per cent of £800 is £80, and 1 per cent is £8.

If you work out what 1 per cent and 10 per cent of your income is, either weekly or monthly, you can fairly quickly see where your present level of giving is, and this will help you decide what the right proportion is for you to give in Gratitude Giving.

Proportionate giving by percentage

	Income	
%	*£80 Weekly*	*£800 Monthly*
1	£0.80	£8
2	£1.60	£16
3	£2.40	£24
4	£3.20	£32
5	£4.00	£40
6	£4.80	£48
7	£5.60	£56
8	£6.40	£64
9	£7.20	£72
10	£8.00	£80
11	£8.80	£88
12	£9.60	£96
13	£10.40	£104
14	£11.20	£112
15	£12.00	£120

And it can continue as high as you wish.

You can work out the percentage proportion of your own income. One per cent of £169 is £1.69, so 10 per cent is £16.90, and 3 per cent is simply £1.69 multiplied by 3, which is £5.07.

You can use this as a guide in your thinking, praying, and personal review to decide your own appropriate level of percentage giving. You decide where on the scale you feel able to begin.

You can also then enjoy the interesting feeling of having money to spend in particular ways which enables you to feel you are, co-operating with God in his mission.

As you grow in the experience of organized proportionate giving, you can consider, with God, whether you stay at the level you began with, or whether you move to a different level after twelve months. No doubt it will depend much upon your faith, your experience of being blessed, and your concern to be generous and grateful.

A giving account

There is a very simple way of handling this for people with a bank account. You can open a charity account, similar to a bank account, with the Charities Aid Foundation (CAF). This is your own account, and you pay into it however much you want to give (but a minimum of £400).

The tax you have paid is recovered and added to the account. You then need only to have one Deed of Covenant, which covers all your giving to whichever charities you choose. If you have several covenants already, this will save you future paperwork. You can easily change over to this system, and the charities receive the same amount from you, but through CAF.

You have your personalized (or anonymous if you prefer) voucher book (which works like a cheque book). You can give to any charity in either regular or occasional payments. CAF was founded by the National Council for Voluntary Organizations. For details about the scheme write to:

Charities Aid Foundation, 48 Pembury Road, Tonbridge, Kent TN9 2JD. Telephone: 0732 771333. Or: Charitable Giving Scotland, 18/19 Claremont Crescent, Edinburgh EH7 4QD.

A mission to engage in

Our exploration of the impact Jesus made on those who heard and saw him, of his teaching and that of the Jewish Torah about attitudes to possessions and to giving, is the necessary groundwork for understanding the concept of Christian stewardship. Money is significant in all this, but it is only part of it, not the whole.

Once we have thoroughly understood the basic concepts, then we can start to see how we and our fellow church members can organize ourselves to plan and implement good stewardship in the whole of our church life. It calls us back to the basic vision of Christian faith and life that we seek to share and celebrate in church.

If you are encouraged at all by this gallop through some of the basics of Christian stewardship, then encourage others to read this book. Meet together to discuss it; pray, and plan ways of making a response in your church. The following chapters offer you some practical ways of doing so.

Stewardship Advisers, or Resources Consultants

There are people available to help you who have a wide experience of helping churches consider the implications of stewardship in their life and witness. The traditional name for them is Stewardship Advisers; the 1990s name for them is something like Resources Consultants.

Your own church directories will have details of local ones you can contact. They are skilled in helping churches take a fresh look at their mission purpose, and in helping them with the whole process of re-examining their vision and practice.

Some advisers/consultants may specialize in the traditional programme that focuses almost entirely on reviewing the financial giving of the church's members, leaving the renewal of vision to come a rather poor second. But most these days have caught up with the vision of the full understanding of Christian stewardship highlighted in the Report from the British Council of Churches. This body has now been superseded by the Council of Churches for Britain and Ireland (CCBI), to which all the main Christian denominations in these islands belong, including the Roman Catholics, who were not members of the British Council of Churches.

The Christian stewardship network of the CCBI provides for an exchange of information, printed material, and expertise between all the Churches. If you want to look at other material besides that offered by your own denomination or diocese, you can trace what may be available through the CCBI Christian stewardship network: The Council of Churches for Britain and Ireland, Inter-

Church House, 35–41 Lower Marsh, London SE1 7RL. Telephone: 071–620 4444.

The Anglican Stewardship Association has a Consulting Team which is experienced in assisting congregations of all denominations in their exploration of Christian stewardship: The Anglican Stewardship Association, 23 Westgate Street, Bury St Edmunds, Suffolk IP33 1QG. Telephone: 0284 753984.

Investment services

For parishes and other church groups, a number of ready and practical services are available to provide professional management for short-term cash and to help protect long-term investments. Among these are the facilities of the Central Board of Finance (CBF) Funds for Church of England trusts and the COIF Charities Deposit Account and investment funds for all denominations.

For further details: The Central Board of Finance of the Church of England, or The Charities Official Investment Fund, both at St Alphage House, 2 Fore Street, London EC2Y 5AQ. Telephone: 071–588 1815.

For further suggestions, see also Chapter 8 of this book.

7

Where are we going?

A congregation whose vision has gone dim often feels rather stuck. Some people like it that way, and resist like mad any suggestions of change. Resistance to change is usually a sign of a frozen faith.

A lively faith, on the other hand, is characterized by a willingness to grow into a deeper faith, love and trust. Growth inevitably involves change. That process is not just an individual, very personal concern, in isolation from other Christians, but is both a personal and a corporate activity.

Change is likely to be forced on a church whose members have lost their vision and commitment. It may come in the form of loss of members, or through economic or political change: it is likely to be painful.

However the Christian experience is that death can also lead to new life in Christ. It is a more important exercise of our stewardship to ask:

'Have we got our vision right?'

than to ask:

'How can we generate enough income to maintain our church as it is now?'

Who gets the vision?

It is important to realize that God gives visions of holiness and faithfulness to his people through the most unlikely folk. Be open to the fact that God may show to you, rather than someone else, his vision for your church.

If that happens, then don't hold back from sharing that vision with others, and working to develop it in your church. Initiatives can come from lay leaders or ordained leaders, and God has no barriers of age, race or gender in giving his visions.

Blocks to such initiative can come from other church members, either ordained or lay. But when we have a vision of what Christ's Church could be, we also have a vocation to do something about it, and not be dissuaded.

Amos was the prophet who forecast that: 'The time is coming, says the Lord, when I shall send famine in the land, not hunger for bread or thirst for water, but for hearing the word of the Lord.'

He was the one who told his people that God hated their religious services, their pilgrim-feasts, and their offerings, and said to them: 'Spare me the sound of your songs . . . instead let justice flow on like a river, and righteousness like a never-failing torrent.'

He was asking them to renew their vision of the godly life, but Amaziah, the priest at Bethel, told him to clear off, and take his message with him.

' "I was no prophet" Amos replied to Amaziah, "nor was I a prophet's son; I was a herdsman and fig-grower. But the Lord took me as I followed the flock and it was the Lord who said to me, 'Go and prophesy to my people Israel' " ' (Amos 7). In this case, God gave the vision to a farmer: the opposition came from the clergy.

It could be you

Usually the initiative will come from the leadership of the church, most likely the vicar, priest or minister. I hope whoever takes the initiative will be able to use the ideas in this book to help members of the congregation understand the whole concept of Christian stewardship more thoroughly.

However, there is no knowing to whom God will give a vision. It is possible that the clergy may be reluctant, perhaps from previous experience of lack of response, to raise this issue in your church. Maybe he or she would be much encouraged if the initiative was taken by one or more members of the church council, or the elders, or deacons, or vestry meeting.

You could be one of the channels through which God speaks. Consider that possibility most carefully.

Each one of us has been given something of the vision, and of the gifts. The Body of Christ can only function fully when each of us plays our proper part in it. This is strongly emphasized by Paul in Romans 12 and 1 Corinthians 12.

A church audit

The seven churches of Asia were given God's assessment of how they were doing in chapters 2 and 3 of John's Revelation. The church at Laodicea was criticized by God because its members were lukewarm. The church at Ephesus was told 'The love you felt at first you have now lost', while the church at Sardis was told 'People say you are alive, but in fact you are dead'.

I wonder what God's appraisal of our church might be? The chances are that he might want a good many things to change, beginning with our priorities and values.

A regular review

This points to the importance for each of us as individuals, and for us collectively as a church community, regularly to review our life, our values and priorities, where we are going, and how far we are achieving the goals we set ourselves in pursuit of the mission-vision of the Christian life. This surely is an essential aspect of good stewardship.

It will involve us in recognizing and repenting of where we have lost our way, or neglected God and his teaching, or allowed the vision in us to grow dim. We can then, with God's help, correct our course, recommit ourselves in his service, and set some goals by which we can evaluate our progress.

Perhaps we can allow ourselves to play God for a day, and day-dream about how we would like our church to be. As an example of what I mean, I offer you my vision of what I would like the church where I worship to become. All of the churches I have worshipped in have had some of these features but none have had them all.

My ideal church

The church is the gathering of the people of God. The key feature of my ideal church is that this group of people, whether large or small, all share a deep sense of gratitude to God for all that he has given us, and a common commitment to love God and to love our neighbour. They thereby exercise good stewardship of the gospel entrusted to them.

Within this fellowship, each individual feels uniquely valued as part of the group, cherished and supported by the others.

It is a real experience of being part of the body of Christ, and sharing our abilities in a co-operative venture, infused with the spiritual gifts of love, faith and hope, which builds up the whole Christian community. It is a church which exemplifies the relationships Paul describes in Romans 12–14, and 1 Corinthians 12–14.

It may be a beautiful building, designed to give glory to God, but it is essentially the place where the church meets. It's more important for the building to serve the people, than for the people to serve the building.

In my ideal church, the congregation value the traditions of an ancient and hallowed building but are able to recognize that it is the mission of the people of God, in worship, fellowship and service, which is a greater priority than even the most valued building.

A building for a purpose

The use of space, furnishings, and decoration within the church, of art, music, movement, liturgy and drama, is flexible and of a high standard, to allow for a variety of means of celebrating and expressing the gospel. These may include facilities for services, for groups of people engaged in prayer, fellowship, education, or service to others, for individual pastoral care, and for administration.

Where the church building does not lend itself to this flexibility, the church leaders plan carefully what supplementary or alternative buildings would most effectively enable the church's mission in that place to thrive.

Worship and faith

The life of this ideal church revolves around a regular pattern of well-prepared and presented worship. The teaching relates the Word of God in the Bible, and the experience of the Church from the early Fathers of Christian teaching to the wisdom and experience of acknowledged Christian teachers in our own day, to a range of current concerns.

This is to build up our members' knowledge and understanding of our faith, our experience of Christian spirituality, and how we live out our faith in the activities and demands of everyday life at home, at work, as citizens, at leisure, and as Christian witnesses. All the members want to grow in their Christian experience, understanding, and spirituality.

The church helps its members face the difficult ethical and moral choices of life today; and to witness to God the Creator, Christ the Redeemer, and the Spirit the Sanctifier, in those many choices and decisions we make each day.

It focuses attention not only on the popular headline concerns of today, such as ecology; personal relationships; health and safety; but also raises less popular issues, such as the appropriate investments for a Christian organization; fair wages for people on low pay; and constructive ways to deal with people addicted to drugs, people who break the law, and people who are violent.

That teaching is expressed in a variety of ways, making use of modern communications, teaching methods and equipment.

Finances and resources

The members of my ideal church individually and corporately plan their financial priorities and choices very carefully. Each one makes a conscious decision after prayerful consideration about how much of their income they allocate as an expression of their gratitude to God. They then take considerable care to direct that money to particular purposes, some to their local church, and some to other destinations.

Similarly, the church leaders responsible for budgeting and spending the church's income, plan their spending on the concerns of the local church and community, and of the wider church and community, with prayerful care.

They are careful about where the church's assets are invested, setting an example in considering the ethics, social responsibility, and ecological practice of the companies in which they invest.

The church as a whole seeks to practise a corporate policy of ecological responsibility: recycling wherever possible; good conservation practice in the church grounds and property; making economical use of fossil fuels with good insulation and fuel economy measures; and buying good-quality materials to last in their equipment renewal and maintenance programme.

Shared ministry

In my ideal church, the contribution of every member is both valued and recognized. The work of mission is seen as the task of the whole body of people, and there is an opportunity for the training and development of many skills.

Sharing the good news with people who do not have a real experience of Christ is not a role restricted to certain people, but is an opportunity that every member has at some time or another.

People occupy particular positions for an agreed and limited period of time, with a cycle of responsibility and freedom. In this way people get the opportunity of serving, leading, and resting, being neither overloaded nor under used.

The special needs of different age groups are met: young children; older children and young people; adults in different age groups: either as single individuals, or as a couple, or as the nucleus of a family with their younger generation of children and older generation of grandparents.

The particular needs of people who are ill, disabled, or carers, people with learning, personality, or relationship difficulties are responded to with sensitivity and practical caring support.

A welcome for all

This ideal church welcomes new members and helps them feel at home as brothers and sisters in Christ.

It gives a particular welcome to people who may be well known in our community for a particular lifestyle, when they come to find Christ and his lifestyle within the fellowship of our church. We remember only too well the radical change Christ brought about in the person originally known as Saul, who, following his experience on the Damascus road, became Paul (Acts of the Apostles, chapter 9).

This applies whatever their colour or racial group. We value everyone as a child of God, treating those who are well-off and those who are poor with equal respect.

Our Lord had a special love for those in his community who were not welcomed by the religious people of that time. We seek to fulfil Christ's commission to receive anyone as we would receive Christ himself.

Outward looking

My ideal church is not an introverted community, but reaches out in joyful celebration, concern, and care to the world around it, and the world at large. It seeks to train and equip its members to play a constructive part as Christian witnesses in their work and community service.

Where members of the church are involved in work, either paid or voluntary, that involves difficult choices, other members of the congregation will support them personally, prayerfully, and when possible, practically.

They will also support members who are very stressed because they work with people who are themselves very stressed by their social circumstances, relationships, or personal difficulties.

There will be opportunities for confidential individual support with counselling, soul-friend partnerships, and a readiness to provide support when an individual is personally dealing with issues of great stress and difficulty which they cannot divulge.

Shared prayer, and respect for others

Its members value the opportunity for shared prayer, fellowship and service with members of other congregations, of our own and different traditions. They seek to learn fresh ways of loving, praying and serving from the different experiences of other Christians.

Whilst retaining our distinctive faith, worship, life and witness, we respect those who seek to travel by different pathways to God in other religions.

We also respect in a similar way those who choose other avenues to enrich their relationships or exercise good citizenship without God. We can learn from them, and be challenged by them, in our stewardship of the gospel, even though we cannot identify with them.

Building bridges in the community

Some of our members have a particular ministry of conciliation, building bridges of understanding and trust between groups in our community who are at odds with each other.

Some also work in the arena of political parties, trades unions, business and professional associations, or voluntary organizations that serve, campaign or support vulnerable people.

All these activities are recognized in my ideal church as a legitimate part of the work of the whole body of Christ, to be supported where the church believes it to be appropriate with prayer, discussion of the issues and priorities, with reference to the insights of biblical wisdom, money, and practical help.

Your ideal church

Perhaps your ideal church is very different from mine. On the other hand, our two views might have many similarities but some important differences. If we are on a journey, it is usually a good thing to know where we are going.

It may be a very helpful exercise for leaders in your church, and in every local church, to take time, consult together (perhaps with some outside and independent person to help, like a Stewardship Adviser), and draw up your own word picture of the ideal church community you would like to develop into. That seems to me to be good stewardship.

Then, having got your compass bearing on your target, you can plan the process for change that will enable you to move towards it. I hope the following chapters will assist you in doing just that.

8

A Mission Statement

We can practise good stewardship, and move ourselves and our fellow church members towards the sort of church we would like to become, if we have a clear goal to aim for. We won't get very far if all we have is a vague notion that 'we wish things were different'.

A leader, or a group of leaders, with a clear vision of what God is calling our church to be, can influence and change thinking and practice amongst other church members. How we try to do it is likely to have a big effect on how far we get.

We may have a great vision, but little sensitivity to other people's thinking and feeling. If so, we are likely to find that a lot of other people resist us and work against us.

Any vision has to be rooted in:

- an understanding of God's truth;
- an openness to God's guidance; and
- a celebration of God's nature.

Resistance to change

People don't want to change something they are familiar with, unless they are very dissatisfied with it. Even if the life of their church at present isn't really what they feel it could or should be, they are likely to prefer what is familiar to the discomfort of change.

Moses found that the Israelites grumbled: 'Leave us alone; let us be slaves to the Egyptians' (Exodus 14), and 'If only we had died at the Lord's hand in Egypt, where we sat by the fleshpots and had plenty of bread!' (Exodus 16).

Change involves a cost. We may want to pay that cost, but the cost may be different for each person in our church. At first, many may regard the cost to them, or to others, as too high a price to pay.

Any leader wanting to respond to a vision of what our church could be, needs to have not only a vision of the church we could become, but also some understanding of the processes by which church members may be helped to share in a commitment to that vision, or some refinement of it.

Biblical characteristics

When we compare the characteristics of Christian life as they are described in the Bible, with ourselves, and our church, we can hardly be satisfied with how things are right now.

There is an excitement in the New Testament about belonging to a church in which people's lives are changed and enriched by becoming Christians.

There is a thrill about a vision of sensitive and loving action, a quality of caring that comes through an encounter with the living Lord. It is quite moving to read in the Acts of the Apostles of the first Christians' generosity, their commitment, their struggle, courage, sacrifice and faith.

Our responsibilities as stewards surely prompt us to review our church life in the light of these biblical characteristics. We need to examine our lives, our goals, and our priorities thoroughly, and invite our fellow church members to do so too.

A momentum for change

Then, instead of just moaning about any lack of vision, faith or love in our church, we can find encouragement from setting goals, working to achieve them, and finding a sense of purpose in what we are doing.

As most of us, much of the time, prefer things not to change, it may be difficult to set that momentum of change going. In recent years, a time of financial crisis in many churches has been the kick people have needed to start to review not just their poor financial condition, but also their poor spiritual condition. There is a strong link between spiritual apathy in a church and apathetic giving.

Some Churches have prepared material to help a local church take a thorough look at where they are, in terms of a vision for mission, the quality of worship, the education and nurturing of members, their levels of giving, and indeed their whole sense of commitment to Christ and his gospel.

Mission audit

The Methodist Church has published *Sharing in God's Mission.*[1] This offers a structure to help leaders enable all their members to play their part in the mission of their church. It is short, well written, easy to read, profound, and stimulating.

The Church Pastoral Aid Society and Scripture Union have published *The Well Church Book*,[2] a practical guide to mission audit. It is particularly intended to help Christians in urban priority areas. Such books are rare indeed.

This well-designed and very readable book is intended for use by church leaders at all levels: Sunday school teachers and community workers as well as elders and church councils, groups as well as individuals.

Mission Pursuit

The United Reformed, Presbyterian, Congregational and Independent Churches have together produced an outstanding pack called *Mission Pursuit.*[3]

This is a thorough and fascinating programme, well designed, with separate sheets in a plastic folder for you to photocopy. This means that everyone taking part can be given their own sheet of paper when each topic is explored. It has a serious purpose, but there is interest and fun in doing it.

The pack helps church members to look anew at their locality, to listen to the hopes and frustrations of people who live there, and to think where God must already be at work, both within and without the church.

It then helps those involved to decide what is the mission purpose of their church, to gather the resources and people to help carry it forward, and to plan and act together.

It is flexible, able to meet the needs of both small and large congregations. It is not a one-off exercise, but enables a church to check progress at intervals. Members can look at what has changed, and what has been achieved. Then the process of looking, listening, thinking, planning and deciding can become a regular part of the church's life.

It could take a long time to work through the whole programme. That might be worthwhile, but equally there could be a benefit in selecting those sections that seem most appropriate, and doing them as a slimmed-down programme. The material is very flexible.

State the problem

Whether or not you use the ideas in these programmes, the starting point for reviewing your stewardship of what has been entrusted to you is to produce an honest survey of the current state of your church.

This should include inviting as many members as possible to share their views on the life, worship and witness of the church. Enabling people to participate in the process at an early stage is likely to help engage their interest, and then their commitment to a positive outcome.

Views can be gathered through discussions in groups, or each individual can write their own response. Some people may want to use both channels to convey their views. What the leaders of the church need to know is:

- What people like about the church's life and witness;
- What they wish was different;
- What they have heard other people admire about this church;
- What they have heard others criticize about this church;
- What needs of the people in this locality the church is meeting at present;
- What needs are not being met.

It is important to stick to people's own opinions in the first two questions. In the second two, it is important to record only what people have said about *this* church. In the third two it is important to look at the needs of a wide cross-section of people, not just those who actually come to church at present.

Look outside our congregation

As God's stewards, we surely have to consider not just the needs of church attenders, but also of those who do not come. Some of these, like carers looking after a dependent relative at home, would like to worship with us but cannot because they have no one with whom to leave the person they care for.

There are some people in every place who are searching for God, for a meaning in life, for friendship, or an opportunity for service. We may not have effectively conveyed to them that we have anything to learn from them and their searching, or to offer them. If that is so, then we need to consider what we should do about it.

From this sort of information, we can build up a more accurate picture of what the problems are. Then we can gather all these views together, and group them into common themes or topics, which the church as a whole can consider at a consultation day.

A consultation day

An individual or small group can be asked to plan a consultation day. People with groupwork or training skills are best suited to planning such a day, rather than someone who happens to hold a particular position in the church, whether ordained or not.

There are specific skills needed to help groups work through a project like this, and not everyone has those skills. We all need to realize when someone else could do a piece of work for us more effectively than we could ourselves.

It may well be better for someone other than the clergy to conduct the day, so that the clergy can participate without also having to run it.

Business organizations will borrow or hire someone with training or groupwork skills if there are none available in their own organization at present. We could take a leaf out of their book.

The objective of the day is to draft a short simple statement that encapsulates the key aims of your church's life and mission, in a Mission Statement.

A Mission Statement

A Mission Statement could be written by an individual or a small group, and then the congregation as a whole asked to comment on it. However this is not likely to produce a Mission Statement that the majority of people feel they 'own'.

There is an altogether different feel amongst a group of people who assent to a draft offered to them, rather than one hammered out by themselves. The section of *Mission Pursuit* entitled 'Decide' offers an excellent way of planning a day's consultation in a church to hammer out a Mission Statement.

The basic idea is simple, but the careful praying, planning and preparation which lies behind the *Mission Pursuit* exercise is the key to its effectiveness.

A day's consultation

What it suggests is having a day's consultation on a Sunday, from late morning to late afternoon, which begins with a presentation of the results of listening to the people. Then folk are encouraged to think about what the mission purpose of their church is today, and what sort of church they would like to become.

The aim is to get everyone involved in trying to find a short form of words that expresses this. The method suggested in *Mission Pursuit* is to have groups of up to sixteen people. Within these groups, everyone divides into pairs and is given a set amount of time for their task. Each pair is asked to discuss and then write down their answers to the question:

What do you believe is the *purpose* of this church in this area?

After that, the pairs combine to form groups of four, who pool their ideas and then produce a joint statement of purpose. Two such groups then combine to produce a joint statement from the eight participants.

The two groups of eight then do the same task back in the full group of sixteen. Finally, these large groups combine with everyone else present at the consultation to see if they can all come up with an agreed purpose.

The leader of the consultation will face quite a demanding task in creating one statement out of all that work. It is important to stick to describing the purpose, and not be side-tracked into working out ways of achieving it. That comes later.

The final result is likely to be a statement of purpose that everyone, or virtually everyone, can feel is theirs. Those who recognize their own contribution are likely to feel even more committed to its message.

Sample statements

It is not a good idea to borrow other people's Mission Statements. It is much more motivating to produce your own in the way I have outlined. The process of producing a statement is more valuable than the end result.

I offer these sample Mission Statements, worked out in different ways, simply to give an idea of what I am describing.

The first is one I offered in 1974 to the church of which I was vicar. I now feel that it was less effective than it could have been because it was drafted by me and I then offered it to the congregation. Perhaps it is also too long. I think it could have been much more motivating, and more memorable, if a shorter statement had been hammered out by us all together.

St Cuthbert's, Ormesby

> We see our purpose at St Cuthbert's to be a family of people committed to Christ and to each other, who together worship God with joy and love, and seek to be guided and empowered by the Holy Spirit.
>
> We hope to know and to care for each other, to support and encourage each other in a Christian lifestyle.
>
> We see it as our task to apply our Christian faith and moral values to every aspect of our lives as individuals, and in our family, social, working and community life. We want to bring others to share our Christian life, and so help them to come to a personal experience of Christ, and their own commitment to him.

Christchurch, Great Ayton

The second example was worked out as a congregational exercise at Great Ayton Parish Church, near Middlesbrough. In this case there was much discussion about the significance of particular words.

> Our mission is to become more visibly a family where our love for Jesus inspires our worship of God, our care for one another, and our service in the community.

Mission purpose

A clear statement of our mission purpose helps us to lose any woolly vagueness about what our church is for, what its work should be, and how we can test whether we are really about our Father's business.

Once it is agreed, it needs to be widely known. It can go as a masthead in the church magazine or newsletter, be printed on service sheets, displayed in the church entrance, and even embroidered on a banner.

The writer of the book of Proverbs tells us that there is 'nothing new under the sun', and there is nothing essentially modern about producing a statement of our mission purpose.

Jesus' mission statements

Here are three mission statements from Jesus:

'The time has arrived; the kingdom of God is upon you. Repent, and believe the gospel' (Mark 1).

'Go therefore to all nations and make them my disciples; baptize them in the name of the Father and the Son and the Holy Spirit, and teach them to observe all that I have commanded you. I will be with you always, to the end of time' (Matthew 28).

'The Lord our God is the one Lord, and you must love the Lord your God with all your heart, with all your soul, with all your mind, and with all your strength . . . You must love your neighbour as yourself' (Mark 12).

A job to do

The Mission Statement has a job to do: to keep everyone's eye on the ball of what we are about. Most Christians have some sense of longing for a quality of Christian life which we all too rarely find.

When we are clear about our purpose, then initiatives can come from various members of the congregation about how to pursue this aim. The statement is not a solution to all our problems, but it can be both liberating and enabling.

References

1   *Sharing in God's Mission: A Programme for a Living Church* (1985). Available from the Methodist Church Home Mission Division, 1 Central Buildings, Westminster, London SW1H 9NU.
2   *The Well Church Book: A Practical Guide to Mission Audit*, John Finney (Church Pastoral Aid Society and Scripture Union, 1991).
3   *Mission Pursuit*. Available from a range of suppliers, including: The United Reformed Church, 86 Tavistock Place, London WC1H 9RT; Presbyterian Church of Wales, 53 Richmond Road, Cardiff CF2 3UP; Congregational Union of Scotland, PO Box 189, Glasgow G1 2BX.

9

Selecting our Aims

Our next task is to identify practical steps by which we can implement our mission. We have to be selective, and decide which are the priority areas at present. This is a task either for a group of church leaders or for the whole congregation.

An individual, or small group of people, should write out a list of possible topics to choose from, with a description of what should be aimed for in each.

Below are some suggestions. There will be other aspects, not listed here, which you may need to consider.

Worship	Spirituality	Relationships
Education	Evangelism	Finances
Buildings	Communication	Team work
Pastoral care	Community life	Stewardship
Ecology	Children	Young people
Elderly people	Family carers	Healing
Music	Liturgy	Doctrine
Social care		

It is not helpful to identify more than eight topics in your final agreed list. You have to be selective. Don't try to think, plan, and act on too many at once.

Any worthwhile change to improve and develop a church needs to be done a step at a time, and prayerfully.

I offer four suggestions for how to select topics. These can be used by an individual alone, or by a group of people praying and discussing together.

Probable, Possible, Unlikely

Have each topic written or printed on paper or card. Give some time to asking for God's guidance, and then invite those participating in the selection of topics to reflect slowly on each topic as they hold the paper in their hand. They may write brief notes on each topic.

At the end of the time of reflection, each person is asked to place their topic papers in their own three piles: Probable, Possible, and Unlikely. When every topic has been allocated, they review the three piles separately. Examine each topic again, and see if it still seems that it is in its appropriate pile. On further reflection we may make some changes.

If a group of people are doing this, they should then discuss until they can agree which topics go in which pile.

Then consider in detail the Probables. If there are more than eight topics for this category, some need removing. If there are fewer, select some from the Possibles. The discussion should aim to be open to other people's perceptions and insights.

If there are two topics vying for a place, we need to consider whether it is appropriate to stop at seven topics, or grow to nine. Two or three topics may combine together to form one.

Visualize Christ in your congregation

This is a prayerful process similar to the one used by the church in Jerusalem, in Acts chapter 6, to choose seven deacons.

Be still and quiet and relaxed. Invite the Holy Spirit to lead your imagination. Picture if you can the members of your church as the crowd surrounding Christ.

See him attending to the particular needs of individuals, and then speaking to the whole congregation: teaching, healing, rebuking, explaining, training and challenging you all. Spend some time with these scenes.

As you let the pictures go, take some time to digest the content of this visualization. Then ask for the Spirit's guidance in the choice of topics, in the light of what you visualized Christ saying to your church.

Share your insights with the others involved in this task, and seek to agree a list of topics.

A gospel exploration

Take one gospel (Mark is short and vivid) and read through it unhurriedly, taking a short section or a chapter at a time. Ask each time for Christ to challenge, inform and guide you, as you seek to know his priorities for your church at this moment. Make your choice of topics when the whole of the gospel has been read.

A group decision

Ask the Holy Spirit to be at work in the process of praying, thinking and sitting through the suggestions, and in the choices and compromises of democratic discussion.

It has been suggested that a committee designing a racehorse would come up with a camel! It is therefore quite important to place our trust in the Spirit's guidance, asking him to illuminate our thinking and our critical processes.

We should guard against too glib an assumption that we have always listened carefully enough when we ask for the Spirit's guidance.

Winston Churchill is said to have remarked of the Foreign Secretary in 1940, Lord Halifax, a devout High Church Anglican, that 'He goes away to pray about it, and comes back with the wrong answer'. Churchill's acid wit may sometimes have a grain of truth in it about our own prayers.

We can sometimes want God's blessing for a decision we have already made, rather than actually asking, seeking, and listening.

The Quaker way of seeking

I wonder if a more tested way of ascertaining God's will for us in our church is to learn from the Religious Society of Friends, the Quakers. They have a long tradition of seeking the guidance of the Spirit by prayerfully asking him to lead them to a common mind.

Each person is asked to say plainly what they think. Anyone who has real misgivings about a decision is asked to voice them, rather than to keep silent. All difficulties can then be considered, explanations or adjustments made, and everyone weighs the issues carefully.

Decisions are not arrived at by majority voting. Only when all can agree is a decision reached, even if that point is long delayed.

Widespread consultation

When a decision has been made about the priorities for action they need to be written up as specific aims. They can then be offered to the membership of the church as a whole. People are invited to respond with criticisms or suggestions. These can be taken into account in drafting their final form.

This becomes an important educational process in the life of the church. The ideas can be discussed and explained in sermons, groups, classes, workshops, or a conference.

A good deal of effort needs to go into making sure that as many people in the church as possible have seen the draft aims, and have been invited to comment on or suggest alterations to them.

The aims can be printed in the church newsletter or magazine, or on a separate handout. All groups and families in the church should be invited to consider them as a corporate activity.

Where families do this, value even critical comment from those family members who do not come to church. Such comments may reflect considerable insight and wisdom.

Clear thinking

Aim to be quite clear about what specific approach, attitude or standard you have in mind for each topic. Getting it into words will help you all to think clearly about what you are trying to do to improve this particular aspect of your mission.

Here are some suggestions for a selection of topics – to be used only as a guide: You must, as a church, select and use your own aims.

Worship

Describe the key ways in which you intend to make your worship a worthy offering to God, drawing upon the skills of as many members of your congregation as possible.

Identify how you will relate your worship in church with your life in the community. Look for ways to identify on-going problems in community life, including people Jesus might today compare to Lazarus in his parable.

Spiritual development

Describe some ways in which you intend to provide opportunities for members of your church to explore the riches of Christian spirituality. Consider organizing a retreat, developing prayer groups, healing groups, or a justice and peace group.

Identify in what way you intend to provide opportunities for group meditation and contemplative prayer.

Identify too what your church might offer to help its members explore the Bible.

Education

Describe how you will develop opportunities for learning in your church. This may be a programme of teaching from the pulpit, in classrooms, adult and junior groups, evening classes, or distance learning for individuals.

Identify what church members, both ordained and lay, will offer to people who wish to become church members. Consider what you will offer to those who ask for marriage, a ministry of counselling or healing, or for baptism and/or enrolment of their children in the church.

Seek to relate the church's plans and programmes of education with what is going on in local schools and adult education establishments.

Pastoral care

Describe your aims for pastoral care (both spiritual and practical) for people who are ill, elderly, bereaved or in trouble.

Identify how this work can be shared among the whole congregation, so that people with particular training and skills can concentrate on helping those in special need of sacramental healing ministry and counselling.

Specify if you intend to train groups of people for particular aspects of this work, and how and when you aim to achieve this.

Social care

Describe the role you see for your church and its members in offering practical care and support, love, prayer and hope, to people who are homeless, poor, sick, unloved, or people who have been victims of injustice, oppression, or neglect.

All of them are people, like us, for whom Christ died, whether they live near us, in other parts of Britain, or other parts of the world. Be clear in what ways you can see yourselves reaching out to those in need, and treating them as if they were Christ himself.

Stewardship

Be specific about the way you will ask people to consider their response to God's generous care, in terms of a loving, grateful commitment to serve him in every aspect of their lives.

Show how this may be expressed in personal commitment and lifestyle, and in giving a proportion of their income to enable God's work to be done in the local and wider communities.

This can also be accompanied by specific aims in pastoral work, and the planned development of the church's whole mission in your area which a more generous level of giving by church members will enable.

It is important in these aims to recognize your duty as a congregation to be careful in investing and spending money, and in using it wisely to further the work of God. It is also important expressly to recognize the importance of prayer before taking decisions, and the need for being open to the guidance of the Holy Spirit.

Communications

Here the aim should be to communicate as attractively and as effectively as possible, to church members and to other people in the surrounding area:

• What you have to celebrate;
• What you are doing; and
• What you have to say.

Identify how to invite people to specific services and events; and how to take something of the joy and the challenge of the Christian gospel to those who have not really considered it, or its implications for lifestyle and moral values.

Consider too what aims you have for improving your communications with your members, being aware of who needs support. If you are embarking on a programme of change, then clear aims for explaining those changes to your own members, and to other people interested in what is going on, are important.

Clear and realistic aims

For each topic selected, you need, as we have seen, a statement which expresses your own hopes and aims. However it is important to walk before trying to run.

In a small church, with few members, the very task of preparing a mission statement and a couple of aims is a major achievement. You don't have to try to choose aims for all the suggested topics.

If it seems right to you and your group just to go for a couple to begin with, then do that, and feel encouraged in doing so. We must be realistic about our expectations. Don't expect miracles to happen by next week! In some churches, just moving forward at all will be a minor miracle in itself.

If we set impossibly high expectations we can too easily become disheartened – but equally, there is little value in setting our aim so low that we can be sure of hitting the target without much change or effort.

Misunderstandings ironed out

Any form of words runs the risk of meaning different things to different people. We may be clear what we mean by our words, but soon find that to other people the meaning is very different.

Part of the value of having written aims is to talk about them, iron out misunderstandings, and get as many people as possible to understand them, even if they do not necessarily agree with them.

Targets and tests

A date needs to be set by which the Mission Statement and the Aims will be officially approved by the church.

They then need to be presented publically:

- explain them;
- celebrate them; and
- offer them to God,

with an act of:

- repentance;
- commitment; and
- dedication,

by the whole congregation.

They can be printed out as bookmarks, to be slipped into prayer or hymn books, Bibles, and books of private devotion.

From then on, church leaders should regularly test how the decisions they make relate to the church's stated mission purpose and aims.

Review them

The church is not tied to them for evermore, because they can be changed if they seem no longer to be appropriate.

It is helpful to fix a definite period, for example, three years, at the end of which the Mission Statement and Aims are reviewed.

You can then decide whether to keep the same form of words, or change them.

10

Helping People Change

Although some people are fearful about almost any change in their lives, most of us have happily accepted the enormous changes in technology and the way of life of this country in the past 60 years. Washing machines, cars, televisions and taped music are just a few of them.

Alexander Pope encouraged us to:

> Be not the first by whom the new are tried,
> Nor yet the last to lay the old aside.

In our attitudes to accepting change, we can perhaps see ourselves in one of these five groups.

- *Experimenters* – who like new ideas, are quite willing to change, will experiment and take risks trying out ideas that may or may not succeed.
- *Adaptors* – who soon catch up with new ideas, but don't want to risk being too much out of step with everyone else. They don't want to be outrageous, but do like to be adventurous.
- *Fashion keepers* – these people take on a change to new ideas and practices when they start to become acceptable. They enjoy being amongst the front-runners with new fashions, ideas or equipment.
- *Cautious adjusters* – are the ones who want to see the effects of change for some time before they adopt new ways.
- *Slow movers* – are very suspicious of change, and adapt only very slowly, and sometimes not at all. As things in life generally are always moving, they either adapt in the end, or become interesting examples of a bygone era.

Changing with care

The ideas I suggest here are not those of an Experimenter, more an Adaptor, or one who keeps up with fashionable thinking. What I have outlined is standard practice even for Cautious Adjusters and Slow Movers in industry, commerce, and education.

So, we have moved step by step through the process of reviewing our stewardship of the gospel, and taking practical steps to prepare to improve our performance. We have identified our Mission Statement, and our particular Aims.

This is one of the easier stages of reviewing our stewardship of the gospel. So far, no one has been asked to make any actual changes.

A strategy

The next part is more difficult. It involves setting a strategy to implement our aims, with specific goals that we hope to achieve by certain dates. But it also involves being quite specific about what is unsatisfactory about our present situation. This has to be spelt out clearly by the key leader, who in most cases will be the priest or minister.

What should be clearly described are four situations:

1   The present situation – and why change is needed.
2   What happens if we don't change – the gloomy picture.
3   The ideal church we want to become – the vision.
4   A situation we could reach in two or three years' time.

This can begin to be unsettling for some people. We all respond to ideas that seem new with a mixture of both thoughts and feelings. We may agree in principle with the need to change, but may not be able to escape from a feeling which we don't always understand, that it is not right, or not comfortable.

Empathy

The leaders proposing change need to empathize with those who are going to be affected. Empathy is standing in the other person's shoes, seeing how it feels like to them, and what it looks like from their point of view.

If you can do that for quite a number of people in your church, then you may be able to help many of them face change more positively.

Any brash enthusiasm you may have will be tempered by understanding their thoughts and feelings. This is likely to help you to propose changes that are more sensitively considered, and more carefully prepared.

That is why it is very important to get people involved in defining the principles of our church life. We are all more ready to consider positive change if we agree in principle that its aims are right. We respond to change according to our own experience of life, our convictions, our feelings, and the way we think.

Discussion at the appropriate level

When new ways of thinking or working are put to us, we may:

- first react with shock;
- then become defensive;
- then begin perhaps reluctantly to adjust our thinking;
- finally adapting to the new ideas.

It matters at what level we are invited to consider new ideas. If, for example, the congregation are told that the monthly family service will from next month be on a different Sunday, at a different time, with a different form of service, many people are likely to react negatively – to grumble, criticize, try to change the arrangements, or stay away.

If, on the other hand, there are a number of unsatisfactory aspects about the family service as it is now, which the church council would like to change for very good reasons, it will be more productive to introduce the idea of change at a different level of thought. Here is an illustration of these different levels in relation to this family service idea.

1 *Conviction* – appropriate worship for families with young children should be provided in our church.

2 *Principle* – this should be provided at a time most of these families can attend, and the form of service should enable many people to participate fully in it.

3 *Idea* – people find it easier to remember the second Sunday each month than the first Sunday, and young people find participating in activity, drama, and music-making engages them more fully in the worship than passive listening.

4 *Strategy* – we have to explain these ideas to those who attend our main morning service, the family service, and those who attend our later service to obtain a wide measure of agreement.

5 *Design* – we have to devise our new form of service, and get agreement from key people, e.g. the leaders of young people's activities, the organist, those we ask to help lead the new format.

6 *Action* – we have to decide when we will implement the changes, prepare those who will take leading roles, and publicize the new arrangements.

If you are thinking about this idea at a different level from the person you are talking with, then you are likely to face a difference of understanding.

Find their level

You may be enthusiastically explaining the action programme to someone who attends the later service before you have discussed any of the other levels of thinking with them. If that happens, don't be in the least surprised to find they don't share your enthusiasm for the idea. They are more likely to if you share your thinking with them one step at a time.

Someone who is quite comfortable with your ideas at the conviction or principle level, can be very uncomfortable at the strategy, design or action level.

Begin at a level they are comfortable with, and work through with them to a level where there is discomfort, and then go slowly and patiently. If you can gain their agreement that way, they are more likely to accept the change.

Boundaries

A very common feature of almost everybody's thinking is that we see boundaries, which may or may not be real.

There is a pen drawing, well known to people who have attended courses on the way we think, which looks like an ink blot. To some people it seems to feature an old lady, and to others a young lady. Some people who can instantly see one, have great difficulty finding the other. The boundaries are in our own perceptions.

There are lots of puzzles which are given to students of human behaviour, to help them recognize the boundaries we impose upon our perceptions by the way we are conditioned to think.

One example is that you are given a diagram of a large square, divided into sixteen small squares, and asked how many squares there are in all. Try it yourself now, and see how many you can find before you look at the answer at the end of this chapter. It will help you to identify your assumptions and boundaries.

Religious boundaries

These boundaries are constraints on our thinking. For church members our boundaries are that we have been accustomed to thinking that only certain ways of thinking, behaving or doing things are appropriate.

Part of the shock which the scribes and Pharisees felt at Jesus' thoughts and actions came from the fact that the boundaries of their thinking were very strictly drawn, whereas his were very wide.

They were shocked because he healed a man on the Sabbath day in the synagogue, his disciples ate corn in the field on the Sabbath, and some of them ate their food without washing their hands. They simply could not believe their ears when he declared to people that their sins were forgiven.

Jesus' difficulty with the disciples focused a great deal on the boundary limits of their thinking.

The whole of Acts, chapter 10 is about how the boundaries of Peter's thinking at first prevented him from taking the good news of the gospel to people who were not Jews. Then, while he was praying, a scene came into his mind which changed those boundaries from then on.

Peter later understood what he had 'seen' and was able to preach to a Gentile audience, who then received the gift of the Holy Spirit. Afterwards he was able to explain his unprecedented action to his fellow members of the church at Jerusalem, who 'When they heard this their doubts were silenced, and they gave praise to God'.

Facing change

It is important that we ask people to consider carefully the constraints on their thinking. There have been enormous changes throughout the long history of the Christian Church. When faced with fresh thinking we need to be open to test the value and the appropriateness of what is suggested.

Step one

In considering change in our church, people will only come to accept the need for it if they are very dissatisfied with what they have now. Many people will perhaps not understand the full situation, and may not stop to examine in what ways we are not being good stewards of the gospel.

Help them see as clearly as possible what are the dissatisfactions with 'now'. This may be in the quality of our worship, the number of our members, or the perceived level of our commitment, spirituality, and service.

It may be a dissatisfaction with our level of financial giving, the quality of our fellowship and congregational life, the fact that we are not engaging young people or families, or that we are not assisting older house-bound members to maintain their fellowship and worship with us.

It is also likely to include our lack of Christian vision, and our lack of application of that vision to the society in which we live, work, and relax.

If we recognize that we need to review our stewardship, then we need to share our sense of dissatisfaction with other church members, rather than impose changes on them.

Step two

A very clear picture of how things could be in our church is needed. It must be realistic, desirable, and attainable.

Step three

Describe what must be done to start making it happen.

Step four

We all need to feel that the discomfort which comes with change – the cost, the effort, the pain – is worth it for the benefits we can gain.

Try to understand other people's concerns, while at the same time moving forward in the process of review and change which has been agreed.

It is not appropriate to give a veto to those who are reluctant or refusing to change, but it is appropriate to try and go forward without leaving a number of people hurt, mystified, and angry.

Change in spite of objections

There are times when, in spite of strong objections, it is felt right by the leadership of a church to make changes knowing that some who disagree will leave rather than accept the changes. That might be the right thing for everyone. Others may threaten to leave in order to try and hold on to power or to manipulate the leadership.

Those unhappy with the pace of change may be able to find somewhere where they can worship, which suits them better. It will be painful for everyone, but sometimes that is the right thing to do.

Their objections may be based either on feelings or on reasoned convictions. Whatever it is, if the leadership of the church feels, after careful thought and prayer, that this is the right thing to do, then they must in conscience take specific steps to realize the vision they have been given.

Where Christians disagree, that disagreement should be faced in a spirit of openness, and of love. That is the spirit that permeates Paul's letters.

Plain speaking from Paul

His letter to the Galatian church is a prime example of his plain speaking. He is astonished to find they are so quickly turning away from the gospel. He reminds them of the differences of opinion in the churches at Jerusalem and Antioch. 'But when Cephas (Peter) came to Antioch, I opposed him to his face, because he was clearly in the wrong.'

He tells them, 'I am afraid that all my hard work on you may have been wasted'. This is to bring them face to face with the need for change in their church, and to help them grow in love.

'You, my friends, were called to be free . . . serve one another in love . . . but if you go on fighting one another, tooth and nail, all you can expect is mutual destruction.' This leads him to remind them that the 'harvest of the Spirit is love, joy, peace, patience, kindness, goodness, fidelity, gentleness, and self-control'.

Plain speaking from Jesus

Jesus too was no stranger to plain speaking. We tend to think that his plain speaking was to those who opposed his ministry, particularly the Pharisees and the scribes. But Jesus also spoke plainly about things some of his disciples found they could not accept. Jesus recognized this, but did not alter what he was saying to conciliate them.

John writes of Jesus describing himself as the 'bread of life', which some of his disciples could not accept. ' ". . . I am the living bread that has come down from heaven; if anyone eats this bread, he will live for ever. The bread which I shall give is my own flesh, given for the life of the world . . . whoever eats this bread will live for ever."

'On hearing this, many of his disciples exclaimed, "This is more than we can stand! How can anyone listen to such talk?" '

'From that moment many of his disciples drew back and no longer went about with him. So Jesus asked the Twelve, "Do you also want to leave?" Simon Peter answered him, "Lord, to whom shall we go? Your words are words of eternal life. We believe and know that you are God's Holy One" ' (John 6).

Breaking a mould

The Church's mission is to grow up in every way into Christ (Ephesians 4). To do that, some churches are likely to have to go through a process of breaking the mould, an experience of pain, even of death, that can lead to new life, vigour, and growth.

Whilst we try to alleviate the pain of those who do not see the need for change, we cannot let them prevent it and so choke the seed of the gospel with the thistles and weeds of human awkwardness, intransigence, or lack of vision.

Try to get agreement

Our aim then is to try to make agreement with our proposed plan more attractive than disagreement with it. We must take account both of people's thinking and of their feelings.

So, to feel ready for change, people need to:

- feel dissatisfied with things as they are;
- have a clear idea of where we are going;
- understand the first practical steps to get there;
- feel the benefits to them outweigh the expected costs.

An agent of change

I hope this does not sound too complex. We have all managed to change things in the past, without having consciously analysed the process in the way I have just done. We may well find on reflection that some of the things outlined, we did without thinking about.

We know that change is possible. Perhaps we realize now more clearly why some of the changes we have tried to introduce in the past have not got very far.

Help from the business world

Business organizations are constantly having to think about change in what they do, and how they do it, and how they can get people to understand and co-operate with it. There are a lot of books on management and psychology that have many good ideas and experiences that can be adapted and adopted in the service of the gospel.

Training departments of large organizations and management courses at local adult colleges can be a fruitful source of fresh thinking and experience from which we could benefit.

However, some of the people who do this work have mental boundaries that make it difficult for them to understand the very different dynamic of a church whose mission is to proclaim, celebrate and live the gospel.

Their thinking about and experience of change, mission, and action plans are likely to be limited to a business culture, in which a product and a profit are the principal objectives. Those in local or national government are likely to be thinking in terms of fulfilling statutory obligations, and find it difficult to adjust to the needs of a church.

An outside helper

One thing business organizations have found from experience that can perhaps help us is that it is difficult for any organization to carry out major changes without the help of an independent person who is not allied to any particular person or group of people within the organization.

It is usually impossible for us to have a clear and unbiased view of how we work and relate to other people in the church. With particular loyalties and friendship, we may be reluctant to suggest something because we think it may upset a particular individual or group.

A person who is genuinely independent can help different groups and individuals to understand their situation, and help them plan to improve it. This is not an outside 'expert', like Sir John Harvey-Jones, who will come in, do a quick analysis and come up with suggested solutions.

An agent of change

An agent of change is more like a counsellor who helps individuals, couples or groups to understand more clearly what is happening in their relationships, how each is behaving, and helps them find ways they find satisfactory to change and develop.

Such a role can be played by Resource Officers or Stewardship Advisers who are able to work in this way; however, not all people in these positions see their role like this. Some see themselves quite specifically as advisers in planned giving campaigns, and they are unlikely to feel comfortable with this sort of exercise.

However there are others who can be invited to help a church in this way. These include church leaders from another church, people (whether Christians or not) who have some skills in group work, training, counselling, or experience in helping change to happen. Some people with such experience in their work place may be both challenged and intrigued to help you work through this process as a church.

Their role and skill

Their role is to look independently at what is happening, to work with you to understand (and help you formulate) what your vision is, and assist you to work out action plans and systems to review your progress.

Their skill is not necessarily in understanding your purpose to start with. It is to help you clearly to state your purpose, then assist, challenge, and support you in moving to constructive change that you (not they) choose.

The change agent can encourage you with compliments, and challenge you with questions. He or she can ask you how realistic your targets are, and whether you are trying to be over-ambitious or unrealistic.

On the other hand, that person can ask questions about whether one of your targets is sufficiently ambitious, or has been set low to avoid the risk of not achieving something difficult.

I hope that such a constructive change agent can be available to each church that seeks to review its stewardship of the gospel in this way.

Perhaps churches of different communions could help fellow Christians in other communions in this way. Both could then learn considerably from each other, and gain much from each other's experience and heritage.

The solution to the square puzzle

If you allow yourself the freedom to recognize that not every square has to be of equal size, you can find 30 squares.

11

An Action Plan

Reviewing our stewardship of the gospel is not a one-off exercise. It is a process of listening, thinking, praying, planning, appraising, and reviewing, to keep moving forward on course.

Navigators plot and chart where they are going, and alter their direction throughout their voyage to ensure that they are not blown off course, or miss their destination. Our aim is to do something similar on our Christian pilgrimage.

The steps of this process that we have identified so far are:

- we have our vision of what Christ calls us to be;
- we listen to God, and to each other;
- we write our Mission Statement;
- we write our aims;
- we understand our role as agents of change;
- we see the value of an outside agent of change;
- we prepare an action plan for our church.

We have described in our aims that we want to achieve certain standards in particular areas of our life and work. Now we need to be quite specific about two things:

(a) the steps we will take, in a certain period of time, towards achieving them;
(b) our degree of commitment to doing so.

Targets and deadlines

There is a great value in setting targets to reach by, say, this time next year. I suggest setting no more than three targets for each aim. It is not helpful to overload people with unrealistic expectations.

That is the quickest way to everyone becoming discouraged and abandoning the whole approach.

People need to be quite clear which of the various important things that they could do, will be done first. They also need to be clear who is going to do what, how it will be done, and by when.

In this way, they have identifiable targets. If they achieve them – great! They can feel they are making progress. If not – they can see how they are progressing, and identify difficulties still to be overcome.

A Christian leader in an American church told me, 'People don't do what you expect: they do what you inspect'. Our own experience seems to confirm this.

We all tend to put more constructive energy and commitment into something that we know somebody – including ourselves – is going to check on a certain date to see if it's done. Even if, like some student's homework, it doesn't get done until the evening before it has to be handed in, it does get done. The deadline makes the difference. That is why we need to choose the targets and the deadlines.

Setting worship targets

Take worship for example – there may be many different things people would like to do.

Targets for developing and improving worship might include rearranging the church interior, introducing new hymn books, developing a music group, and teams of readers and worship leaders. They might also include a review of the teaching content within worship, the themes explored in sermons and in other ways.

A crèche might be needed, and ramp access for wheelchairs and people with walking difficulties. Perhaps sound amplifiers are needed to help everyone hear clearly, and a few copies of the prayers and hymns in Braille and Moon to assist people with visual handicaps.

It could be that there is a need to provide space for silence at times in some services, and to help people understand more fully the meaning of each part of the liturgy. People might want to introduce some material from the worship of Taizé or Iona, or to include classical choral pieces composed for cathedrals.

Worship and relationships

Another church might want to develop a much more open, relaxed, charismatic feel to worship, with joy, praise, liturgical dance, personal testimony, healing, and personal one-to-one sharing within the context of a service of prayer, praise, and ministry to each other.

People might want to focus on the themes of repentance and forgiveness, with a careful preparation for saying the general confession, and perhaps a liturgy of penitence in Lent and Advent.

In another church, people might want to have some elements of the above, as well as a training programme for servers and lay members to assist in the distribution of the Communion. They might want a series of special services – like a mass for children, or worship on the theme of prisoners of conscience, or peace and justice.

Seasonal worship

Some people might suggest that our harvest thanksgiving be changed to include the products of local manufacturers and craftsmen as well as farmers and gardeners.

Worship for the great seasons before Christmas and Easter might feature modern liturgical material for Advent and Lent, preparing in each case for a dramatic presentation of the nativity or passion of Christ.

We might want to hold a retreat or pilgrimage as part of the process of enriching our understanding of our participation in worship.

Outreach

Other people will want their worship to reach out to people who do not worship with them now. Open-air services, or services at the beginning or end of a March for Jesus, may be their aim.

There may also be a need for a big education programme on understanding worship, and what each person puts into it and gains from it.

Setting dates

It is important to identify our priorities. This may include doing things in a certain order to help people adjust to change, and deciding what needs to be changed by what date.

All of the changes suggested here will endure better when they have been thoroughly thought through. It is better to discuss them fully so that snags or consequences you have not at first considered are taken into account.

So, setting targets should always allow for consultation, explanation, and adaptation at a pace that most people can cope with. Moving forward at a pace that most members of the church can move at, is both sensible and sensitive.

Select priorities

Again, priorities need to be selected. This time in two different groups. In the first, identify what you consider to be:

- most important,
- important,
- less important.

Then decide:

- longer-term goals, to be achieved in say two, three or more years' time;
- short-term goals, to be achieved in six or twelve months.

Next:

- set target changes and dates;
- identify who is to be responsible for taking initiatives to achieve each target;
- decide what resources are needed: people, training, cash, and equipment.

If you have a target, and insufficient resources, perhaps you need to identify a time by which you aim to obtain the resources, then set a target date after that for your hoped for achievement. The targets must be realistic.

Annual review

The leadership of the church will need to review every year how far these targets have been achieved. You may find that you have done much more than you expected in some areas, and not achieved your targets in others.

It can be very helpful to invite your outside independent agent for change to participate in this review. She or he can then help you to look for the reasons why these results have come about.

From this, you may on the one hand get much encouragement, and on the other hand you may learn to handle disappointments. Such learning may bring you to revise your aims or targets, and the methods you will use to achieve them.

You may well be imitating Robert Bruce's spider, trying again and again until you succeed. On the other hand, your agent for change may ask you to consider whether what you set out to do is still worth aiming for, or whether from this experience, you should choose a different target.

An annual service

This process of review could helpfully be linked to an annual service whose theme is a renewal of our commitment to Christ and his gospel. The Methodist Church has its annual Covenant Service at New Year, when this theme of self-examination, repentance, re-dedication, and commitment to Christ in the coming year is a powerful and moving experience.

Some years ago, I attended a most impressive Stewardship Service at a Baptist church in Modesto, California, on the evening before Thanksgiving Day. It was a service of praise to God for all the blessings they had received.

During the service, many members of the congregation came to microphones in different parts of the church and shared in an uninhibited, and what seemed to me typically American way, their own personal experiences of blessing during the previous twelve months.

The congregation then committed themselves afresh to the Lord for the coming twelve months, each worshipper having made a tangible expression of gratitude and commitment in a pledge of money for God's work in that church. It was an invigorating and joyous occasion.

A tangible commitment

This illustrates a difference for many of us in the way we think of commitment. Many Christians think of their act of commitment as a once-, or perhaps twice-in-a-lifetime act.

We committed our lives to Christ in the service of God and our fellow human beings at our baptism, or confirmation, or when we were admitted to full membership of our church or the Society of Friends, or enrolled as a fighting soldier in the Salvation Army.

But there is a need to give a regular account of ourselves. We shall of course each of us be required to give an account of ourselves to God at the end of our earthly life. Meanwhile, we need to review our stewardship regularly; the most appropriate period is once a year.

The pattern of celebration in the year provides us with particular occasions when there can be a natural focus on self-examination, repentance, assurance of our forgiveness, and then our re-dedication and commitment. The Bible contains many instances of God's people needing to do this. The prophets, histories, and Psalms are full of them.

Josiah's review

In the reign of King Josiah, the people had been (rather like some of us) so busy with worship and repairing the church, that they had got out of the practice of actually reading God's Word. Their whole practice and values were terribly adrift from what God was wanting of them.

While the Temple was being repaired, someone found the scroll of the law. When they brought the scroll to the king, and it was read out, the king 'tore his clothes' in an act of repentance, and ordered his court officials 'to go and seek guidance of the Lord for himself, for the people, and for all Judah, about the contents of this book that had been discovered'.

Reading the Word of God brought Josiah to repentance, reform, and a renewal of the covenant with God on his own part and on behalf of his people.

The sense of fresh commitment was clearly a memorable experience: '. . . no Passover like it had been kept either when the judges were ruling Israel or during the times of the kings of Israel and Judah . . . No king before him had turned to the Lord as he did, with all his heart and soul and strength, following the whole law of Moses; nor did any king like him appear again' (2 Kings 22 and 23).

Our stewardship appraisal

Our annual stewardship appraisal could well focus on the Mission Statement, and our aims and targets. This could be part of the preparation for some particular occasion, like the renewal of our baptismal vows at Easter, or the annual Covenant Service, or the development of our harvest thanksgiving into a General Thanksgiving for all God's gifts.

The theme of the readings in the Alternative Service Book of the Church of England for the eighteenth Sunday after Pentecost also provides an apt occasion, celebrating The Offering of Life (Deuteronomy 26.1-11, Nehemiah 6.1-16, or Ecclesiasticus 38.24-end; 2 Corinthians 8.1-9 or 1 Peter 4.7-11; Matthew 5.17-26 or 25.14-30).

Any of these occasions would be an appropriate time to:

- review our belief, in a re-examination of our statement of faith, like a catechism, creed, or confessional statement, or a gospel or other book of the Bible;
- review, as a church, our stewardship of the gospel, and identify which of our targets we have achieved, which still seem appropriate to our mission purpose, and to identify our targets for the next twelve months;
- thank God for his blessings to us in the past year, and express our repentance, our 'turning round', and our request for his forgiveness, blessing and guidance as we go forward;
- express our gratitude and commit ourselves to specific personal targets for personal prayer and Christian education, service, style of life, and financial giving.

Most of us are not used to doing any of these things. That, I suggest, is poor stewardship on our part. We neither account to God, nor to ourselves, for what we believe, how we seek to walk in the footsteps of Christ, and how much our belief means to us in the tangible values of money and personal offering.

There is great value to us all in rekindling a spirit in our Christian life of offering sacrifices to God.

Sacrifice

Sacrifice in the Old Testament is an expression of gratitude and devotion to God. It was offered in the form of a choice animal from the worshipper's herd. No blemished animal was worthy of being offered to God. So the offering itself was costly.

The principle of sacrifice was identifying the life of the person making the offering with the animal to be offered. This life was then offered to God. For the Israelites, the life of the animal was in the blood, and it was this life which was offered. In the same way, Christ's blood was shed as he gave his life in costly offering to God for our salvation.

The Old Testament also stipulated that God's people were to

give one-tenth of their annual wealth to God. This was an act of gratitude for all that God had given to them, but it was also to pay for the priests, the services, and later the Temple. In addition there were a number of offerings for particular occasions, either thank-offerings or sin-offerings.

Generosity and blessing

Tithing and sacrifices did not stand alone, as the sum of what God called his people to do and be. He gave them the Torah, the sacred law, which as we can see in Exodus chapters 20 to 23 ranged over every aspect of daily life; treating justly people who were poor or vulnerable; punishing people who treated their slaves badly; giving appropriate behaviour for people involved in a quarrel; hygiene laws; and warnings not to spread baseless rumours.

The self-disciplines of love and justice go together with worship and with sacrificial giving in the Old Testament. Neglect one, and you soon find the others neglected too.

It is also the experience of Christians that where people have given sacrificially, of themselves and their possessions, in thanksgiving to God for the whole of what they have, they are truly blessed. God is generous to us. Those who give generously are blessed generously.

This is why it is also important for a church to give a proportion of its own income to further other aspects of God's work outside its own limits, that it may be both a means of blessing and thereby receive blessings.

12

Personal Appraisal

Life in Christ is life-enhancing, but when the vision fades, the commitment slackens, then love grows cold.

We are looking afresh at our Christian vision, with a readiness to change. This change is not a vague desire for things to be better, but a move as determined as that of King Josiah to be enthused by the Word of God, and do something creative about it.

Change can happen in our church at three levels:

- in the individual
- in the group or team
- in the congregation as a whole.

Growth and development can begin at any or all of these points. It can be welcome, or threatening, to people.

The speck and the plank

If we have very clear ideas about how other people need to change, but do not recognize our own need for it, we shall not be effective stewards of the gospel.

In the Sermon on the Mount, Jesus gives us a humorous example to tease us about this very point. There is this Christian who can see the tiny speck to criticize in someone else, but does not notice the much greater fault in himself.

The humour, I find, is in the picture of me trying to look at the speck of sawdust in my brother's eye, and all the while failing to notice the enormous plank sticking out of my own. It makes me think of a Gerald Scarfe cartoon, with the exaggerated plank blocking the Christian's line of sight (Matthew 7).

Begin with me

Not only will it help our church to have its action plan, it will help each of us to have our own individual one. There is a telling little prayer that asks:

> Lord change our world;
> Lord change our nation;
> Lord change our church;
> Lord begin with me.

When someone makes a conscious choice to become a Christian, there is a new beginning for them. I remember my own experience of making such a decision at the age of seventeen. In preparing for my baptism, and then six months later my confirmation, I was very conscious of making new beginnings. I thought about the way I thought, prayed and behaved, very carefully at that time.

Personal review

It is partly the recollection of how significant and meaningful that was, that has drawn me in recent years to want to make a personal review of my life in relationship with God, my wife, my family and friends, the people whom I seek to serve, and my colleagues at work.

I know that unless I make some conscious effort at a systematic review, I am likely to drift along with good intentions but no accurate examination of whether I am carrying out my good intentions.

The American who said 'People don't do what you expect, they do what you inspect' had some pithy wisdom. I reckon we each of us will only do what we expect we will do, if we inspect what we have done.

Steering a course

A personal annual self-examination and appraisal is something I suggest we each consider doing as part of our preparation for the annual review of our mission in our church congregation. I was taught when I became a Christian that I should carry out a weekly self-examination before receiving communion.

That was a tight discipline, and it tended to focus on negative things like sins – what had I done wrong? I stopped doing it so often after some years because it became too routine, and it was always so negative.

I much prefer the metaphor of steering a course which requires regular adjustment and correction, because that can build on the positives, and keep the negatives in proportion. In a regular time of self-examination and personal review, listening *to* God should feature more strongly than talking *at* him.

Gratitude can play the larger part, and repentance takes a proper though less prominent place. This leads to renewed commitment and a request for God's grace to help move inward, forward, upward and outward.

Such a regular practice is a helpful preparation for an annual self-appraisal. This can be done either alone, or in consultation with someone else – your spouse, a friend, a counsellor, a spiritual director, a confessor, a soul-friend.

Support group

I am fortunate to belong to a confidential support group with whom I can consult on this. We are four ordained people, two women and two men. We seek to learn from each other about different perceptions of ministry, and to support each other in our life and work.

Any Christian can gain much strength and insight from exploring with a small group of fellow Christians, in a confidential, supportive and non-judgemental (though sometimes quite challenging) group, our experiences and perceptions of being a Christian in today's world.

We have to be careful, as in other things, to keep our focus on our mission, our purpose for meeting. So we have to be open with each other when we are inclined to chat rather than keep our eye on the ball.

The value of doing a self-appraisal with friends in a regular support group, where the others do a similar exercise, is that it can help each member. Just the fact of opening yourself up to trusted Christian colleagues, who in turn open themselves up, can be both supportive and liberating in the Christian life. It is not an inquisition, but an exercise in honesty and self-awareness.

A solo exercise

Not everyone can form a support group. Not everyone has even one person they can trust to help them in their self-appraisal. We can do it as a solo exercise, though I think we are likely to find that we are more self-critical and less supportive with ourselves than a trusted Christian counsellor might be with us.

Whether or not we have someone to share our self-exploration with, the first steps we have to do alone.

1 It is important to create times for silence, for prayer and reflection, at home, at church, or in the open air, as a preparation for your annual self-appraisal. Listen to the Word of God in the scriptures, and the voice of God within you. Seek to understand both yourself and his will for you.

2 Write a character description of yourself. Pay attention to both positive and negative aspects of yourself of which you are aware.

Be prepared to like yourself as well as to give yourself a prod or a rebuke. The value of writing such a description is that our thoughts then become quite specific rather than vague feelings and intentions. The process helps us to learn things about ourselves.

3 Write down five events or experiences in the past year that have been significant for you. Also identify any changes you have made, or wish to make, in the way you think, feel and behave, arising from those events or experiences, and from your listening to God.

4 Review your relationships with God and with specified individuals. As you know a lot of people, it is unrealistic to try to review your relationship with all of them.

If you think about 'people in general', you lose the testing examination of your relationships with particular individuals. Looking at your relationships with one or two people will give you many insights that may be relevant in your relationships with lots of others.

Part of your appraisal process will be to decide how many people in each category you will consider. For instance you might specify your partner, three members of your family, three friends or colleagues, two people who receive help or a service from you, and two people you find it difficult to relate to. You choose both the numbers and the categories of people for yourself each time.

So, review your relationship with:

God
Your partner
Other members of your family – how many?
Friends/colleagues   – how many?
'Customers'   – how many?
People you find difficult   – how many?

Write down your observations about your relationship with each one. One observation I found myself making recently was that I was so busy doing things for God that I didn't spend enough time relating to him.

5 Discuss what you have written with your trusted individual or group, or reflect on it alone.

6 Then reflect further, to enable you to decide on your own specific goals and priorities for the coming year under four headings:

- Personal development
- Personal relationships
- Personal tasks
- Personal discipline

7 When you have these clear and written down, you will probably find that the most helpful structure for you is some opportunity to offer them formally to God, in a simple prayerful act, either alone, or with the person or persons with whom you have shared your explorations.

In this time you can express praise and thanks, repentance, a request for forgiveness and for grace to nourish you in sensitive, Christ-like love, in a renewed commitment and a fresh start.

Perhaps in your church people could be provided with the opportunity of a corporate liturgical service in which to express all these things to God. A period of silence for people to offer their individual aims to God, in something akin to the Methodists' Covenant Service, can be a joyous opportunity for corporate dedication and commitment for the coming year.

Personal development

If we are to 'grow up in every way' then we need to develop as individual Christian souls in our character, our personality, our sensitivity and spirituality. You hear some people say that having reached a certain age 'they are not going to change any more'. That is not the experience of those who want to change and grow, or those thrust into new situations.

We grow into new and more demanding jobs. We are changed by experierices of trauma, poverty, suffering, and those experiences that give us an insight we didn't have before. Many people have changed their diet or habits or become ecologically aware in response to new information and understanding.

People's lives have always been changed by an encounter with the living God. New knowledge, new insight, a new experience of love, an experience of acceptance and forgiveness can transform us.

God of Surprises

A book I have found particularly helpful for personal development and can gladly recommend is *God of Surprises* by Gerard Hughes.[1]

The former BBC Religious Affairs Correspondent, Gerald Priestland, a Quaker, describes this book by a Roman Catholic Jesuit priest as 'one of the great books of spiritual guidance'. It is a joy to read, loving, gentle, sensitive, spiritual, and thoroughly biblical.

Our commitment to personal development is likely to feature specific ways in which we intend to explore the riches of spirituality, worship and biblical exploration, using our imagination, understanding and will, and the sacramental means of grace given us by Christ. So we need to be specific with ourselves and God about what we intend to do about each of these aspects of personal development.

Personal relationships

The heart of our Christian experience is in relationships. Our understanding of God is of love in relationship: Father, Son and Holy Spirit.

'God is love; he who dwells in love is dwelling in God, and God in him . . . If someone says, ''I love God'', while at the same time hating his fellow-Christian, he is a liar . . . We have this command from Christ: whoever loves God must love his fellow-Christian too' (1 John 4).

'Love must not be a matter of theory or talk; it must be true love which shows itself in action', John writes in the previous chapter. So it is essential to our spiritual health and well-being that we look at our relationships with other people.

If there are gaps and blind spots in our loving, we are told by Christ in the Sermon on the Mount to identify them and deal with them before we offer our gift at the altar.

Again, a general intention will not carry us very far: it is the specific intention to develop particular aspects of our own nature, and of our relationships with specific individuals, that will help us most to grow in love and show it in action. We need to agree with ourselves and with God, which aspects of our relationships we intend to work at in the coming twelve months.

Personal targets

Many jobs around the house we have promised to do only get done when the motivation is strong enough. Lists, deadlines, or frequent reminders may help focus our motivation, or wear down our resistance or inertia.

As before, we may not do what people expect us to do, but we will usually get round to doing what they inspect. We pave the way to our own hell with our good intentions that never get realized in actions.

If we set our own targets for the work we do in our different roles – at work, at home, at church, at leisure, in service to others, and in things we hope to achieve – we give ourselves something specific to aim for. We can then measure how effective or successful we have been.

It is important to set realistic targets; neither impossibly ambitious nor too many of them, so that we are constantly placing ourselves under intense pressure to achieve. That said, most of us achieve more working under pressure of some sort.

If we are selecting our own targets, then they should be taxing enough for us to give of our best, yet not cause us to become more preoccupied with tasks than with personal development and relationships. Eager beavers are likely to need help to wind down their targets, whilst sluggish laggards are likely to need help to raise their sights.

Personal discipline

Many years ago, the Archbishops of Canterbury and York produced a short guide to the duties of church membership. A report on Christian Stewardship to the Church of England's General Synod in 1990, *Receiving and Giving*,[2] recommends that an updated version of this be widely used 'as a guide, rather than a requirement, for new and existing members' of the church.

That guide stated:

'All baptized and confirmed members of the Church must play their full part in its life and witness. That you may fulfil this duty we call upon you:

- To follow the example of Christ in home and daily life and to bear personal witness to him.
- To be regular in private prayer day by day.
- To read the Bible carefully.

- To come to church every Sunday.
- To receive the Holy Communion faithfully and regularly.
- To give personal service to church, neighbours and community.
- To uphold the standard of marriage entrusted by Christ to his Church.
- To care that children are brought up to love and serve the Lord.
- To give money for the work of the parish and diocese and for the work of the Church at home and overseas.'

An adaptation

I have used their structure and order in suggesting the following points to consider in framing your own personal discipline. If you find it helpful, I suggest you try to write some specific intentions for the coming twelve months, which you keep in your Bible, or a devotional book, so that you can refer to them regularly – perhaps monthly.

- We have our unique part to play in the life and witness of our church.

    What do you see your part being in your church now?
- We have the opportunity to reflect the light and love of Christ in our lives.

    How do you see you can do that in your activities, decisions and relationships each day?
- We are invited to share each day of our life with God.

    How do you intend to safeguard time to listen, love and share with him each day?
- We are offered the Word of God in the scriptures.

    How do you plan regularly to read and seek to understand the Bible?
- We have the opportunity to share in worship and fellowship with other Christians each week.

    How often do you plan to do this?
- Christ invites us to his table, to be fed with the sacrament of his body and blood.

    How often do you intend to accept his invitation?
- Christ asks us to 'always treat others as you would like them to treat you'.

    How do you plan to express that in service to others?
- Marriage is intended as a lifelong partnership of love.

    How can you help to nourish this ideal in your own relationships, and how can you help others to do so?

- Christ has a special love and protection for children.

  How do you aim to nourish and protect the spiritual, emotional, social, educational, and artistic well-being of your own, and other people's, children, and help them to know Christ's special love for them, and to experience the joy of knowing him?

- Christ invites us to store up treasure in heaven, rather than treasure on earth.

  What proportion of your income will you decide to give this year, as an act of gratitude to God for all he has given you, that you may help to do his will on earth as it is in heaven?

References

1   *God of Surprises*, Gerard W. Hughes (Darton, Longman & Todd, 1985; ISBN 0-232-51664-2).

2   *Receiving and Giving: The Basis, Issues and Implications of Christian Steward-ship* (GS 943; published by the General Synod of the Church of England, Church House, Great Smith Street, London SW1P 3NZ, 1990).

13

Relationships

So far this book has been action-focused: a doing book, rather than a being book. For many of us, the most significant experiences of our Christian life have not been on the journey outward, of public worship, acts of compassion, or church organization, but on the quiet inner journey of exploration: the soul's journey into the wonder of God.

All our religious busyness is so much froth, unless we are rooted in God. As Christian stewards we have a responsibility for the nurture of souls, our own and others'.

Christian spirituality is related to the rest of our life. It is the process of developing richer relationships with God, and with other people; our contribution to those relationships is what we shall consider now.

Mutual relationships

This is not an exploration of self-centredness, to get spiritual treats for ourselves. It is an invitation to mutual relationships that grow, deepen, and are enriched, as we recognize and understand ourselves, and give ourselves to the other person or people.

It is a call to love God with heart, soul, mind and strength, and our neighbour as ourselves.

'Love one another', writes John, 'because the source of love is God . . . God is love; he who dwells in love is dwelling in God, and God in him . . . We love because he loved us first. But if someone says, "I love God", while at the same time hating his fellow-Christian, he is a liar' (1 John 4).

Spirituality and relationships are intertwined. The way we are, and the way we relate and respond to other people, is shaped by our inherited nature, by our experiences in childhood and adult life, by our beliefs and training, and by our concept of ourselves.

All these give us 'oughts' and 'shoulds' in our life. They programme us into behaving in certain ways, without us necessarily examining whether our thoughts, feelings and behaviour are rational, appropriate, or really loving.

'The child is father of the man'

A woman who felt really loved and valued as a child has a foundation for personal growth and development, for mental health, good relationships, motivation and self-discipline.

A woman who did not feel wanted, loved, or valued as a child, who could never please a demanding parent, who was subject to much criticism and punishment, but almost no praise, will carry that feeling of being of little worth into her adult thinking and relationships, with God and with people.

A man who felt very overshadowed by his older and more able brother, and who tried unsuccessfully in different ways to gain recognition or to do as well as his brother but never managed it, will carry the burden of that unequal relationship into his thoughts, feelings, relationships and prayers as an adult.

His elder brother may well carry an exaggerated sense of his own worth, based on his knowledge and skills more than on any warmth, sensitivity, and integrity in his relationships.

Guilt and anxiety

A child who grew up frightened of God, fearing divine retribution for minor sins, may well become the adult who has a highly pronounced degree of guilt and anxiety, and great difficulty in feeling there can be any valuable relationship between him or herself and God.

When the minister preaches about guilt and repentance, the same message will be heard very differently by these adults.

The message 'Love your neighbour as you love yourself' may sound glorious harmonies in the minds of those who grew up with strong bonds of love and affection, but there will be discords and flat notes in the minds of those who have never yet learnt to love themselves.

Pastoral sensitivity

This is an aspect of Christian stewardship which in my experience is very rarely addressed in sermons and general teaching to adult Christians. It is usually ignored in preparation for adult commitment in baptism, confirmation, church membership or ordination, and is rarely addressed even in spiritual direction.

The art of pastoral care of each other, and of individual souls, is a much needed ministry in our churches. People cannot just respond with knee-jerk reactions to standard Christian call-signs.

We can all be helped on our spiritual journey of exploration if these experiences of our earlier years are recognized as significant to every dimension of our life, including our relationships with God and with other people.

Healing wounds

In many cases these memories and experiences have left deep wounds which need healing. There are few pastoral counsellors or psychotherapists who are able to help Christians explore that journey in both religious and personal terms.

I hope that the Association of Christian Counsellors,[1] and the new lease of life being given to the Association for Pastoral Care and Counselling,[2] will help to develop a much more effective ministry of Christian pastoral care in Britain.

A congregation is a group of unique individuals, not a mass-produced brand of pew-fillers. We each have our own life-story that we bring to Christ; he deals uniquely with each one of us.

He is the good shepherd, he calls his own sheep by name; he knows them, and they know him. He leads and protects his sheep, unlike the thief who comes only to steal, kill and destroy: 'I have come that they may have life, and may have it in all its fullness' (John 10).

Our individual experiences of pain and trauma, love and cherishing, of rejection and desertion, of being sought and valued, are interwoven in our prayers and relationships. If we are to 'grow up into Christ' (Ephesians 4) then it will be important for us to find ways of exploring and understanding ourselves, and the experiences that have shaped us up to the present time.

It will also be important for us to find ways in which our wounds from childhood can be healed.

Stages of development

It is also important to realize the opportunities to be found at important stages of development in our lives, and in significant changes of relationships. Leaving home, beginning a marriage or other partnership, becoming a parent, taking on different responsibilities at work, becoming a grandparent, taking on community responsibilities, retirement, are all changes which have potential for growth.

Changes in any of these relationships – separation, divorce, bereavement, estrangement, a major illness or accident, moving house or job – have considerable social, psychological and spiritual significance.

The stewardship of life involves considering the constructive and destructive elements in these experiences, and finding opportunities for personal growth towards the fullness of Christian maturity and experience.

This is the subject of whole books, and many of them. I cannot do justice to it in one chapter in a book on Christian stewardship and renewal. I can only point to writers who are addressing these aspects of the stewardship of personal growth and development.

These include aspects of the ministry of healing of childhood traumas, of personal growth and development, contemplative prayer, and Christian maturity. The selection is personal, and offered in the hope that you will be helped to begin to explore this aspect of Christian stewardship and ministry more thoroughly from here on.

The Road Less Travelled

The Road Less Travelled: A New Psychology of Love, Traditional Values, and Spiritual Growth is a very readable book. It is divided into four sections, headed 'Discipline', 'Love', 'Growth and Religion', and 'Grace'. It is written by M. Scott Peck, an American psychiatrist who is a Christian of considerable wisdom, insight and sensitivity.

He has some fascinating things to say about the nature of loving relationships. He offers us help to recognize true compatibility, to distinguish dependency from love, and to grow in both self-confidence and sensitivity.

He is concerned that we increase our self-understanding through facing our difficulties and working through the painful changes that are necessary for us to grow to new life, greater love, and the freedom of living with and for Christ.

It is publicized as a No. 1 International Bestseller; so you are as likely to find it on the station bookstall as you are to find it in a religious bookshop.[3]

Original Blessing

Original Blessing is described as a Primer in Creation Spirituality. It takes us on a spiritual journey in which we are invited to celebrate the beauty of the earth and of human creativity and relationships; to be open to, but not overwhelmed by, our pain; to use our creativity to create rather than destroy; to value love more than fear; to value the feminine as well as the masculine in religion and relationships.

The author, Matthew Fox, is a Dominican priest, and another American. He challenges the notion that our spirituality should centre on the doctrines of the Fall and Redemption. He emphasizes the doctrine of Creation, which he believes has been almost entirely overlooked as a religious perspective with strong historical and biblical roots.

It is a much harder read than Scott Peck, but is a book which can be explored for a lifetime of growth in personal and spiritual relationships.[4]

Heaven in Ordinary

Heaven in Ordinary: Contemplative Prayer in Ordinary Life brings us back to an English author. It is a delightful little book by Angela Ashwin. It is not hard to read; most chapters are just two pages long. Angela Ashwin offers her insight and experience of learning how it is possible to live prayerfully, centred in the stillness of God, when our days are full of activity and noise.

She makes full use of the ordinariness of daily life, including our feelings of being unworthy. She starts straight in, responding to such feelings as: 'How can I even presume to try and live prayerfully when I spend all day feeling exasperated and critical about the people I work with?'

Other objections include 'I'm too old to start praying now', and 'I've done nothing but shout at the children all day. I would feel a hypocrite if I sat down and prayed now'. She offers ways in which a busy and harassed person can live a life of prayer. She looks too at how we look at life, at pain and failure, and what we can offer. It is a valuable and practical way in to a deeper experience of prayer.[5]

Stewardship of life

I hope that the idea of Christian stewardship no longer seems to be the description of a church fund-raising campaign. Christian stewardship is the stewardship by Christians of the whole of our life.

We are indeed stewards of our money and possessions, but 'life is more than food, the body more than clothes', said Jesus. 'Set your mind on God's kingdom and his justice before everything else, and all the rest will come to you as well' (Matthew 6).

Here is a vision in which we may change and be renewed as we prepare to celebrate the end of the second Christian millennium. I pray that God will bless you richly as you seek to exercise your stewardship.

References

1   The Association of Christian Counsellors, King's House, 175 Wokingham Road, Reading, Berks RG6 1CV. Telephone: 0734 662207.

2   The Association for Pastoral Care and Counselling, c/o The British Association for Counselling, 1 Regent Place, Rugby, Warwickshire CV21 2PJ.

3   *The Road Less Travelled*, M. Scott Peck (Arrow Books, 1990; ISBN 0–09–972740–4).

4   *Original Blessing*, Matthew Fox (Bear & Company, Santa Fe, New Mexico, 1983; ISBN 0–939680–79–3). Distributed in Britain by Element Books Ltd, Longmead, Shaftesbury, Dorset SP7 8PL. Telephone: 0747 51339.

5   *Heaven in Ordinary: Contemplative Prayer in Ordinary Life*, Angela Ashwin (Mayhew–McCrimmon Ltd, 1985; ISBN 0-85597-380-3).

14

Doing something about it

Some books you read and put on your shelf, and then you pass on to the next one. Others you wear out with repeated use. I hope you will want to wear this one out, making full use of the ideas, suggestions, and starting points to explore certain aspects of Christian life in more detail. This chapter simply offers you suggestions for doing this.

You can use this book on your own, as a basis for your personal review of your Christian commitment and response, if no one else in your church seems willing to do so. You could of course do what I do with certain books: buy a second copy to lend to others and so spread the ideas, while I am able still to use my own copy at home.

There is likely to be a better basis for stewardship and renewal in your church if you start a group of people to read, think, pray and discuss possible ways forward.

The content can be used as the basis for a renewal programme in the church as a whole, seeking to involve all the members in the process. Or it can be divided up into sections, for use as a syllabus for sermon programmes, adult education courses, workshops, a retreat, a series of renewal days, a house group programme, or a Bible study course.

Individual stewardship and renewal

Journal

You have read the book once. The chances are that there are many things in it that made some impression on you, but then you read on. It is also likely that there are things in the book which did not register with you on your first reading; they may help you to think more perceptively about your life and your faith if you come to them a second time.

One way which I think could be very helpful is to use an exercise book; begin a journal of your thoughts and reflections, your hopes and prayers. Read this book again, with your journal beside you.

Stop whenever something strikes a chord with you. Listen. God may be speaking to you, but if your mind is so busy moving on to the next thing, you won't be listening to him. Think, reflect, mull the idea over in your mind. Allow God to develop your thoughts and speak to you.

Then write in your journal your thoughts, your feelings, your responses. It is important to write not only your thoughts, but also to describe your feelings and articulate your responses.

We clarify a lot of our thoughts when we put ideas into spoken or written words. We communicate more effectively with ourselves when we can go back another day and consider what we wrote at the time.

Write as much or as little as you like. Use it as a means of exploring something of your own reactions to the words of Christ or the prophets, to Paul, John, James, Peter, or any of the other writers quoted.

Your own response

Perhaps you might write your own personal mission statement and aims (Chapters 8 and 9), and your considered response to the suggestion for updating the Archbishops' Guide to the Duties of Church Membership (Chapter 12). Make your own response to the ideas on proportionate giving (Chapter 6).

Consider your reaction to change (Chapter 10), and write in your journal of how you have dealt with significant change as you developed from childhood (Chapter 13). Explore your relationships, with other significant people and with God.

Choose one or more of the books referred to as your next step, such as those by Richard Foster (Chapter 5) or Gerard Hughes (Chapter 12). Maybe you will find it helpful to continue your journal as you move forward in Christian development.

Your journal can also be where you collect favourite prayers, quotations, and ideas to explore further, and where you can write about your thoughts and feelings generally.

There is an excellent book of ideas on how to use a journal for self-guidance and expanded creativity. It is *The New Diary*, by Tristine Rainer.[1]

Soul-friend

Exploring such ideas with a trusted friend or small group is a very valuable way of developing in the Christian life. You can perhaps provide mutual support to each other, or you can meet regularly with a Christian of experience in growth and development whom you consult. Explore with that person your thoughts, prayers, and feelings, and your ideas for ways forward for you.

Individual retreat

You could use this book, and your journal, as the basis for an individual retreat. You go somewhere where you can be quiet and prayerful – it could be a religious retreat house, or it could be any place to stay.

What is important is that it is somewhere you can be quiet and give time to relaxing, praying, reading, a little gentle exercise like walking, but without other distractions like television, people who chatter, or work to be done.

You have time to look at ideas with some unhurried consideration. You can dwell perhaps prayerfully on some of the Bible passages. You might spend time reading the whole of one gospel.

You might find that your own sense of ways forward for your renewal, growth and development emerges very clearly in your retreat.

Group stewardship and renewal

The Church began with a group of twelve people whom Jesus chose as the foundation for his mission. Renewal in the Church has always been developed by groups of Christians who have shared a vision of renewal, and enabled each other to move forward to act upon it.

The monastic Orders, the Methodist movement, the renewal of the Church in Latin America since the 1950s, the House Church movement, the Charismatic movement, have all grown through a network of Christian groups.

This subject is explored fully in *The Liberation of the Church: The Role of Basic Christian Groups in a New Re-Formation*, by David Clark.[2]

This offers a comprehensive review of the role of basic Christian groups in shaping the Church of the future.

Your ideal church

Individual Christians can take initiatives in forming renewal groups, you don't have to wait for someone in authority to either give permision or take the initiative. Look again at Chapter 7. The single objective for your group could be, having all read this book, to write your own description of your ideal church. Then consider what you feel led to do about taking some initiatives to try and develop those characteristics in your own church. In doing so, consider very carefully Chapter 10, 'Helping People Change'.

The subject of 'My ideal church' (see Chapter 7) could be the focus of a study programme in your church initiated by the clergy, elders or church council. It could be a series of six or eight weekly meetings, drawing on various elements of this book, or the focus for a renewal day or weekend.

Study programme

A number of subjects in this book can be used to form the syllabus for an adult education series, a training group or house group. Alternatively, Richard Foster's *Celebration of Discipline* is divided into three topics with four subjects in each. It makes an excellent syllabus for twelve events. If every participant is able to buy their own copy, you have the makings of a thorough programme for exploring aspects of Christian spirituality for today.

Similarly, this book can be used as a syllabus for groups of Christians to explore the issues of stewardship, using Chapters 1 to 7, 12 and 13.

A word of caution: there is too much content for each chapter to be dealt with in one evening, unless every participant has read the chapter and the person facilitating the group can help it identify one key issue from the chapter to consider on each occasion.

Setting a Mission Statement

You can use one chapter on its own as the focus for a study programme. Ideas for setting a Mission Statement (Chapter 8) could be used for a day-long workshop at your church, or a series of group meetings over several weeks.

In setting a Mission Statement there is great value in getting a high proportion of the congregation together to work at it on one day: progress seems more encouraging in one day than if it takes several weeks.

Congregational stewardship and renewal

To explore these ideas with the whole congregation you may need to begin with a small group of people who might offer leadership in exploring them more widely in your church. It may be that you begin by meeting with some person from outside your congregation like a Stewardship Adviser, Resources Officer, Missioner or Evangelist. They can help you consider some of the issues, and the process by which you do so.

Use this book

The groundwork can be laid by using material from this book in sermons, talks, and church magazine articles. If you sell copies of the book in church people will be able to realize more clearly what is being talked or written about.

It can certainly make a big difference to spreading the word if a vigorous effect is made to sell the book in church over a period of weeks.

Even in churches which do not have a regular bookstall, investing in ten copies to sell or lend to members of the congregation can help raise the level of awareness and understanding of the issues being considered in the church stewardship and renewal programme.

You could invite people to read the book a chapter a week, and use the Sunday sermon to draw out issues from the week's chapter, and to point to ideas, issues or themes in the coming week's chapter.

Sermon notes

An excellent way of helping people to retain more of the sermon than we usually do is to provide an A4 sheet of paper, folded to form an A5 leaflet. On this print your headings, key points and Bible references, spaced throughout the four pages so that there is room for people to write a brief note of things they particularly wish to remember.

Print details of further reading at the foot of page 4. We all take a more intelligent interest when we are encouraged to take notes.

It may seem a bit strange to take notes in church – but if we are concerned to make the most effective use of communications methods then we have to consider imaginatively how we all learn best.

The leaflet outlining the sermon, and the additional notes we have added, can then be taken home and used as a reminder of what we heard, a stimulus to explore the subject further, and an aid to doing so.

Borrowing people

Borrowing a group of people from another church, to come and share with members of our congregation their experience of working with some of these issues in their church, can be quite a help.

Inter-change between urban and rural parishes, or between people from similar types of parish, can be very fruitful in helping both sides to learn from each other, and in the process, make new Christian friendships.

The borrowing can include consulting with people who specialize in adult and child education, to get some modern and imaginative ideas for communicating Christian teaching in our church. These people may or may not be Christian.

If you can ask some people – like an industrial training officer, an art therapist, an advertising specialist, a skilled teacher – to advise you on how best to communicate whatever you wish to do, you will get a variety of ideas and techniques.

These people may not be members of your church, or even Christians, but their technical ability may be of great value to the work of your church if they are willing to consider carefully the subject you want to communicate, and can offer some ideas on how to do it.

Annual stewardship review

Consider the idea of an annual review of your mission and stewardship as a church: see the action plan in Chapter 11. This could be linked, as I suggest there, to some Covenant Renewal Service, or to the observance of Lent.

Alternatively, you could develop the Harvest Thanksgiving into a much broader concept of a Celebration of Thanksgiving, including not only the fruits of the earth but other fruits – spiritual, artistic, educational and social – as well.

This could be linked to a corporate activity in which every church member is invited to prepare by making their own individual review, using some of the ideas in Chapter 12 on personal appraisal.

Then the celebration can be of both thanksgiving and recommitment after careful examination of our stewardship of the gospel, of our relationships, of our lifestyle, possessions and giving, of our spirituality, and of our citizenship.

Over to you

This is as far as we go in this book. The next steps are in your hands.

I was told that when the American troops were moving through France after the Normandy landings, a group of tanks reached a village after some heavy shelling had damaged the church. A soldier who went in found a statue of Christ: the hands had been knocked off.

He wrote a label and hung it round the neck of the figure before returning it to its stand. The handless statue of Christ then declared: No hands but yours.

References

1   *The New Diary*, Tristine Rainer (Angus & Robertson Publishers, 1989; ISBN 0-207-95964-1).
2   *The Liberation of the Church*, David B. Clark (1984; ISBN 0-946185-05-0). Available from The National Centre for Christian Communities and Networks, Westhill College, Selly Oak, Birmingham B29 6LL. Telephone: 021-472 8079.